THE NEW PARAPOLICE
Risk Markets and Commodified Social Co...

Policing in a capitalist economy operates on both state and private levels. Much of the existing literature on private policing assumes that the private sector is oriented almost exclusively toward loss prevention and does not fulfil a crime-control function. In this carefully researched study, George Rigakos considers the increasingly important role of the 'parapolice' in the maintenance of social order. He argues that for-profit policing companies adopt many of the tactics and functions of the public police, and are less distinguishable from the latter than has been previously assumed in the criminological literature.

Rigakos conducted a detailed ethnographic and statistical case study of Intelligarde International – a well-known Canadian security firm – and uses his results to investigate the following: How are discipline and surveillance achieved organizationally and commodified as 'products'? How do security agents themselves, and those they police, resist social control?

This work has wide-ranging theoretical implications, drawing on Foucauldian concepts such as risk, surveillance, and governmentality and on Marxian formulations of commodity and aesthetic production. The first criminological ethnography of a contract security firm in Canada, this book will be of interest to criminologists, sociologists, lawyers, and policy-makers, and to any non-academic reader with an interest in the experience of those employed in the parapolice.

GEORGE S. RIGAKOS is Assistant Professor in the Department of Sociology and Criminology at Saint Mary's University in Halifax.

THE NEW PARAPOLICE

Risk Markets and
Commodified Social Control

GEORGE S. RIGAKOS

UNIVERSITY OF TORONTO PRESS
Toronto Buffalo London

© University of Toronto Press Incorporated 2002
Toronto Buffalo London
Printed in Canada

ISBN 0-8020-3562-0 (cloth)
ISBN 0-8020-8438-9 (paper)

Printed on acid-free paper

National Library of Canada Cataloguing in Publication Data

Rigakos, George
The new parapolice : risk markets and commodified social control

Includes bibliographical references and index.
ISBN 0.8020-3562-0 (bound)   ISBN 0-8020-8438-9 (pbk.)

1. Intelligarde International – Case studies.   2. Private police – Case studies.
I. Title.

HV8099.C33T67 2001   363.28'9'0601   C2001-901963-7

This book has been published with the help of a grant from the Humanities
and Social Sciences Federation of Canada, using funds provided by the Social
Sciences and Humanities Research Council of Canada.

The University of Toronto Press acknowledges the financial assistance to its
publishing program of the Canada Council for the Arts and the Ontario Arts
Council.

University of Toronto Press acknowledges the financial support for its
publishing activities of the Government of Canada through the Book
Publishing Industry Development Program.

Contents

Tables and Figures

Tables

Figures

Acknowledgments

I would like to thank all of the men and women of Intelligarde International, and especially Darrell Hayward, for allowing me into their lives – they made this book possible. Although Intelligarde president Ross McLeod and I harbour fundamental political differences, I have no doubt that he supports this research and the production of knowledge in all its forms. Instead of raising obstacles of the type most criminologists have come to expect from police managers, Mr McLeod was a keen facilitator of this research. I thank both him and his *parapolice* – a term I have borrowed from him for the title of this book. I would also like to thank Desmond Ellis, Michael Overington, Margaret Beare, Barbara Hanson, Livy Visano, Walter DeKeseredy, Leo Davids, Regina Schuller, and John McMullan for their help with earlier versions of this material. I also appreciate the assistance of Veneise George and Colleen Lightbody, who helped me sort through mountains of files. Stephanie Duncan at the *Toronto Star* was an invaluable source of information. Additional thanks to Clifford Shearing and Philip Stenning and to Virgil Duff and Chris Bucci at University of Toronto Press. Thanks also to Matthew Kudelka for his rigorous copy editing. My deepest thanks go to Ruth Murbach, editor of the *Canadian Journal of Law and Society*, for granting me permission to reproduce sections from 'Bubbles of Governance: Private Policing and the Law in Canada' (2000), 15(1): 145–85, written with David Greener. Also, to Nico Stehr, editor of the *Canadian Journal of Sociology*, for permission to reproduce sections from 'Hyper-panoptics as Commodity: The Case of the Parapolice' (1999), 24(3): 381–409. My thanks to Alex Smith for his photography and to Intelligarde for allowing me to purchase the pictures that appear in this book. Finally, thanks to Anne for being my escape.

THE NEW PARAPOLICE

Introduction

On my first ride-along with Intelligarde, the Law Enforcement Company, I accompanied a quality control manager while he investigated an allegation that one of his security officers had used excessive force. He spoke to a working-class Romanian man in an arm sling who had been injured during the ordeal. The supervisor was sympathetic, and clearly bothered by the incident and immediately set about finding who was responsible. As we walked toward the elevator he turned to me and admonished, 'This isn't what private policing is about.' He was referring to the heavy-handed measures of his fellow officers.[1] Of course, he was only partly correct. While some of my preconceptions of Toronto's most talked about security force had been confirmed by this incident, I soon came to understand that I was missing the very big picture. As I examined the existing sociological literature on public and private policing, it quickly became apparent that while many important aspects of private security were already well understood, just as many were not. In this book I consider the broader political, social, and theoretical issues revolving around the practice of 'parapolicing' in Toronto.

This Study in Context

After an extensive literature review I could not locate a single published study of private police that examined the *doing* of security work from the perspective of line officers. So in part, this project adds to the literature by providing the first ethnographic account of a private security company in the tradition of past qualitative works in the general sociology of policing (e.g., Manning, 1997; Manning and Van Maanen, 1978; Skolnick, 1966; Westley, 1970). I extend past ethnographies of policing into the business of security. This is not to suggest that past researchers have ignored the swelling ranks of security officers in Canada. However, they have relied almost completely on surveys to produce demographic data on security officers (Erickson, 1993; Shearing, Farnell, and Stenning, 1980) instead of direct observation of private police mobilizations. Because they have looked from the outside in, instead of assessing the internal dynamics of private policing, the information they have gathered about the function and role of the private police has often reflected the attitudes of outsiders such as corporate managers (Shearing, Stenning, and Addario, 1985a), the public police (Shearing, Stenning, and Addario, 1985b), and the general public (Shearing, Stenning, and Addario, 1985c). In the ethnography that follows I reverse this tendency by making the attitudes of private security officers the centre of analysis. Thus, for instance, I ask the parapolice of Intelligarde to comment on management tactics, their relations with the public police, their interactions with the general public, and their opinions of how the media represent their work.

Until now, scholars of the private police have maintained a distance between themselves and their object of analysis. Social control theorists and theoretical criminologists have astutely observed the important role that the private police and private justice systems play in maintaining social order and resolving conflicts (Christie, 1993; Cohen, 1985; Henry, 1983). Yet rarely have these analyses been anchored to observations of private policing in action. A notable exception is Shearing and Stenning, who in their analysis of the 'Disney order' (1987b) excavated the mundane rituals and routinized procedures of maintaining surveillance and linked them to extant theory.[2] Having directly observed the processes by which social control is maintained, and having analysed the official documents, procedures, work rules, and work environment of Intelligarde International, I hope in this book to extend existing theory. How is compliance achieved? How are eviction and banishment handled? And how are the private police disciplined and surveilled as they control others? The answers to these questions cannot be gleaned from approaches that do not employ direct observation and interaction with street-level officers and managers.

Objectives of This Study

In conceptual terms, this book has two major thrusts: descriptive and theoretical. By descriptive I mean that I am providing a case study of a private policing organization, not previously available in published studies. In particular, I am providing information pertaining to (a) the everyday work of private security officers at Intelligarde, (b) the occupational culture of Intelligarde security officers, and (c) the demographics of those officers, as well as their attitudes toward the police, the public, the media, their work, their managers, and other security companies.

Thus in this book I am following a necessary exploratory agenda for a nascent area of research. Private policing began receiving academic attention in the late 1970s, but published findings in this area are still sparse, and relatively few scholars are involved in the research. Little has been done to record arrest statistics, or the demographic composition of people detained, or the characteristics of private security firms, and this in itself constitutes good reason to do so now. But it isn't the primary reason: I am concerned mainly about extending (and departing from, where necessary) existing theory about the subject.

The theoretical foundation for this book is based on four criminological discourses: 'risk society' (e.g., Beck, 1992b; O'Malley, 1992; Simon, 1987), governmentality (e.g., Burchell, Colin, and Miller, 1991; Foucault, 1991a; O'Malley, Weir, and Shearing, 1997), Marxian (e.g., South, 1988; Spitzer and Scull, 1977; Weiss, 1978), and pluralist (e.g., Shearing, 1992; Shearing and Stenning, 1983). There is much overlap among these four literatures; the first two in particular are deeply intertwined. This book is thus heavily indebted to a broad range of previous thinking on private policing. Each of the four literatures has something unique to offer the subject of private policing. Specifically, risk society, governance, and pluralist discourses illuminate the processes of surveillance and discipline that are inherent to social order in late modern capitalism. Each of these three describes corporate logics extensively and promotes an understanding of actuarial practices as the privileged formula for making populations 'known.' I add, however, that none of these approaches pays sufficient heed to the overriding profit motives of private security firms. To understand how private security works, Marxian conceptions of commodification and fear must be added to the analysis (Spitzer, 1987; Loader, 1999). Private contract security firms do not engage in social control for its own sake – it is obvious, but often ignored, that they have a financial incentive to organize their businesses using corporate and panoptic templates. The task for the 'risk markets' perspective I sketch in Chapter 1 is to uncover these processes.

Recent thinking has effectively blurred the dichotomy between public and private policing (e.g., Kempa et al., 1999; Rigakos, 1999; Bayley and

Shearing, 1996). Very little can be understood about the function, organization and mandate of policing bodies when we overemphasize the importance of these sometimes arbitrary legal designations (Rigakos, 1999). The new parapolice both reinforce and frustrate previous theorizing on the private police. They are the epitome of private actuarial decision-making and 'loss prevention' governmentalities (e.g., Shearing and Stenning, 1982b; O'Malley and Palmer, 1996; Shearing, 1992); yet at the same time they embrace retributive logics and operate in such a way as to 'at base' commodify their surveillance apparatuses. This has hardly been considered in past theoretical analyses. This is what makes Intelligarde International such a rewarding case study: the organization strives to perfect the often analysed panoptic tendencies and surveillance practices that contemporary postmodern social theorists find so fascinating, but it does so for reasons largely beyond the scope of these theorists' analyses. Ironically, Intelligarde's aspirations are demystified most effectively when we utilize the very modernist Marxian orientations that such latter-day thinkers seek to overthrow.

Organization

In Chapter 1 I examine previous theorizing on the private police and recent developments in the sociology of policing. I explore the connections between critical and 'governmentality' discourses as they affect analyses of the police. I deconstruct recent 'risk society' approaches as well as more dated Marxian interpretations. The perspective I take attempts to fuse critical and poststructural theoretical applications, with the goal of understanding the modern manifestations of contract private security politically and emotionally charged 'risk markets.' How do contract security organizations conduct surveillance, and why are they charged with these responsibilities? What changes in the structure and ideology of neoliberal risk markets have given these initiatives legitimacy? I argue that modern parapolicing is organized around the fetishistic desire to commodify security and manage risk. This process is fuelled by late capitalist actuarial logics that *simulate* surveillance while simultaneously *selling* it.

Chapter 2 outlines the methods I employed in this study: critical ethnography, formal interviews, and archival research. These multiple investigative approaches mesh with the book's descriptive and theoretical objectives. In the formal interviews I conducted I focused on the negotiation between surveillance and resistance by examining the attitudes of both managers and line officers. The interviews clearly establish the culture of 'crime control' among Intelligarde employees, who work under conditions of 'perpetual dread.' I reveal the embedded, commodified nature of parapolicing and show that the mundane procedures of private law enforcement and surveillance are products of actuarial rationales. This fulfils my mandate to provide a first-hand account of parapolicing. Ethnography strongly informs the combative relations between Intelligarde security officers and the populations they police. The archival materials – occurrence reports, personnel files, internal documents, media reports, and the bannings database – measure statistically the crime control function of the parapolice and thus their marketability in late capitalist risk markets. The materials also provide information about Intelligarde's personnel and practices.

In Chapter 3 I begin my analysis of the new 'parapolice': a security company that explicitly attempts to bridge the gap between the public and private police, increasingly rendering the distinction more and more meaningless from an analytic perspective. They constitute the vanguard of the emerging risk markets of urban fear and neoliberal rationales. I then explore the powers of the Intelligarde parapolice of Toronto, and conduct a statistical analysis of their routine mobilizations and compare their activities with those of the public police. Finally, I take the reader on what one of the officers called 'a trip through the sewer' – a patrol of Intelligarde sites in the Sherbourne and Dundas area – as an introduction to the functions of the parapolice.

In Chapter 4, I continue my exploration of Intelligarde by examining the company's recruitment, pre-employment testing, and training practices. I consider the destabilizing effect of new recruits on the culture of parapolicing before providing a statistical profile of the security staff at Intelligarde International: the Law Enforcement Company. Finally, toward the end of the chapter, I begin to consider issues of race, class, and gender as they play out both within the company and in the external politics of parapolicing Toronto's inner-city neighbourhoods. It is here that I first discuss the allegations of excessive force and racism that have been lodged against the company by the Toronto media and by various advocacy groups.

In Chapter 5 I catalogue the hyperpanoptic characteristics of Intelligarde's surveillance system as they affect both the security officers doing the monitoring and those who are being monitored. At this point I set aside the dialectic of control and resistance that is inherent in all systems of surveillance, and entertain the fantasy of total control and perpetual examination that is embedded in the physical and virtual architectures of panopticism. Most importantly, however, I reconnect this *virtual* system to the very *material* necessities of selling surveillance in late modern risk markets. While there is nothing new about selling policing and the skill of making 'unruly' populations 'known,' the virtual ordering, digital representation, and fluidity of information exchange makes the process qualitatively different.

In Chapter 6 I take up the modes of resistance employed by both Intelligarde staff and subject populations to avoid detection within the Law Enforcement Company's hyperpanoptic surveillance system. I introduce the reader to modes of routinized resistance such as the art of 'ghosting,' and to more *base* responses to the 'police machine,' including mob justice and 'swarmings.' I then describe Intelligarde's occupational culture of fear and mutual assistance as facilitating an often romanticized mercenary 'legionnaire' quality. This revolves around feelings of isolation, reliance on fellow officers, and the perceived abandonment by the public police and community.

ONE

Theorizing the Private Police

In this chapter I review extant theorizing on private policing and social control by dividing the literature into four overlapping areas. I begin by discussing Marxian orientations, which see the private police as instruments of class domination and as tools for maintaining a disciplined labour force. I then consider approaches which eschew notions of 'state centrality,' and which argue instead that the private police are best understood in the context of an integral plurality of state and corporate interests. Because the next two discourses I identify – 'risk society' and governmentality – are often linked in the literature, I consider them in tandem. Each of these models of inquiry makes a unique contribution to our understanding of the private police and social control; however, each also has its limitations. Toward the end of this chapter I attempt to transcend these theoretical constraints through a 'risk markets' orientation that I have formulated specifically in order to understand the parapolice.

Private policing has been receiving more and more attention from academics in part because of its tremendous growth. If there is one truism about private security, it is that the sector has expanded considerably in the postwar era (Cunningham, Strauchs, and Van Meter, 1990; Kakalik and Wildhorn, 1971); in the United States, there have been more private than public police since around 1977. Private policing has continued to grow since then (though this growth has tapered off in the last decade) to the point where today, private security agents outnumber the public police by approximately three to one in the United States (Cunningham, Strauchs, and Van Meter, 1990). In 1994 over 100,000 people were employed as 'watchmen' or guards in Canada. Over 19,000 of these were licensed security guards in Ontario (Leclair and Long,

1996: 15).[1] Also, there were 1,641 dual security guard/private investigator licence holders operating in Ontario. The 1991 census reported that there were 61,500 police officers and 104,800 security guards in Canada; by 1998, according to more recent statistics, there were only 54,722 public police but over 109,900 guards and watchmen. This means that the private police now outnumber their public counterparts by at least a two to one ratio in Canada (Swol, 1998). As the number of people employed in private security increases, so will academic interest in this social phenomenon (e.g., Kakalik and Wildhorn, 1971; Shearing, Farnell, and Stenning, 1980; Shearing and Stenning, 1982a).

The concept of 'police' has historically been linked to the idea of the city-state itself (the word is derived from the Ancient Greek πολυς, meaning city), and with the later notion of safety and security (Shearing, 1992). But 'policing' has evolved to include a wide variety of social controls that encompass both private and public techniques of governance (Knemayer, Shearing, and Stenning, 1987a). As the private security sector increases in size relative to the public police, it becomes more and more important for us to understand how the state's role in policing is changing at the same time.

Marxian Approaches

There are two predominant Marxian notions in the study of the private police: there is an instrumental understanding of the state as a 'managing committee for the bourgeoisie' (e.g., Couch, 1981; Klare, 1975; Weiss, 1978), and there is a structural understanding of the state as a place on which to focus when analysing developments in private policing (e.g., South, 1988; Spitzer and Scull, 1977). By either approach, the role of the state is at the centre of analysis. It is undeniable that private police have been deployed in the past as 'private armies' to suppress labour. Especially in the United States, there is plenty of evidence that early private police forces consisted of little more than gangs of ruffians and strike breakers who were hired by overzealous firms such as the Pinkerton Detective Agency, or consolidated into quasi-public bodies such as the coal and iron police (see especially Couch, 1981). Clashes between striking labourers and paid pugilists often led to bloodshed. There is much to be learned from these critical analyses. Most Western democracies accepted varying degrees of state-sanctioned private policing under the direction of industrial interests. Unlike the United States, however, Canada and England quickly mobilized public, federal police in lieu of reluctant local constabularies; the purpose of these new bodies was to quell anticapitalist worker revolts and Native revellions, including (in Canada's case) the Métis Rebellion. Private agencies similar to the railway police and the coal and iron police in the United States existed in Canada and Britain alongside the North West Mounted Police and the Metropolitain Police of London, but they were less violent than their American counterparts, except with the early exceptions of Winnipeg and Estevan, in Canada (see Brown and Brown, 1973). In sum, the 'iron fist' of oppression (Cooper et al., 1975) was flexed by élites, industrialists, and landowners quite often in the United States, and with the blessing of the state, but far more rarely in other developing nations of the time.

Instrumental approaches do not help explain why private policing has changed over time. Today's private security companies have little involvement in anything resembling the suppression of organized strikes, although there are notable exceptions.[2] On the contrary, the vast majority of social control exercised by the private police is accomplished with the compliance of subject populations and is organized far outside the purview of state intrusion. Shearing and Stenning document this clearly in their examination of the 'Disney order' of policing (1987b). Visitors to Disneyland are not subjected to coercive measures aimed at controlling them; rather, they pass through myriad controls aimed at maximizing their enjoyment and minimizing risks, and avoiding litigation.

The instrumental Marxian tradition, from which some earlier studies emanate, may well explain how private security began to develop around the time the American labour movement was taking root, and why the state actively endorsed private armies and 'Pinkertonism'; but it cannot really explain the multifarious nature of security arrangements in late modern capitalism. This is especially true when we consider that working Canadians often pool their funds or use their authority as elected members of tenants' associations to 'choose' heavy-handed security firms (such as Intelligarde). Ironically, in some cases the security companies that Canadians hire to protect their homes are the same ones that police their places of work. Marx had very little to say about the need for security outside direct production, yet commercial and residential settings are now the predominant sites of private security deployment. Clearly, the private police do considerably more than pacify labour.[3]

Other state-centred formulations fall into similar traps. Some Marxian approaches have described a process of state–police relations that goes beyond unidimensional, instrumental notions. Spitzer and Scull

(1977), have suggested that policing – specifically, the state's role in mediating between private and public policing – evolves in three stages. In the first stage, capitalist development erodes the basis for traditional forms of social control, in tandem with changes in the mode of production.[4] In the second stage, the established capitalist state begins sharing policing costs by inaugurating a public domestic force. This is done, the authors argue, because it is more attractive than private arrangements for facilitating legitimacy and promoting 'false consciousness' among labour. In the third and final stage, a state fiscal crisis results in policing responsibility being redistributed to large corporations 'to guarantee profits and secure an environment for uninterrupted growth' (1977: 27). This formulation regards the state as a 'legitimizer': the decisions it makes are counter-intuitive to individual capitalists, but at the same time are necessary for capitalism to succeed.

The 'relative autonomy' of the police from the state is most clearly articulated by South:

> It is a commercial compromise between the sovereignty of the state, which constitutionally represents the status quo, and those sections of society whose commercial interests are most benefited by the maintenance of that status quo. In accommodating the development of the private security sector with whatever mixed degrees of caution or enthusiasm, the state is not simply 'saving money.' It is not reducing its commitment to more social control intervention – economically or politically. It is, at one level, acceding to a new (or at least renewed) dimension of capital's assertion of its relative autonomy from the state. (1984: 190)

Accordingly, whether we view the advance of privatization as creeping laissez-faire capitalism, a crisis of state budgets, or racially inspired stigmatization (see Johnson, 1976), the police (both private and public) have their own distinct interests and agendas, but they nonetheless collude with the managing committee of bourgeoisie to promote an environment for profits and economic growth. According to South (1984: 109; but see also South, 1987; 1988), the private police provide a 'buffer' function for capitalist interests. In portraying themselves as neutral arbiters in law *enforcement*, the police disguise the political motivations behind law *enactment* and, for our purposes, the organization of policing itself. Like instrumental models, relative autonomy perspectives make the state the focal point of analysis for understanding the police. Johnston (1992: 210–14) has criticized this tendency for limiting our understanding of the multidimensional nature of both the state and the police. It is assumed that at core, state interests are fixed and ever-constant: the state seeks through whatever means possible to advance its own preservation and, by extension, the capitalist order. These Marxist formulations, however, raise doubts about the state–police relationship – doubts that may not be entirely answerable using relative autonomy or instrumental conceptions.

It is, in my view, dubious for Marxist analysts of the police to ignore the fact that contract private security firms operate to realize a profit. Marx himself said comparably little about the state per se; he was more concerned about how capital was organized – specifically, about the mechanisms by which value, price, and profit operate. In this sense, most Marxian analyses of the police have not seized hold of Marx's greatest contribution to knowledge. For example, no one has sufficiently explored the similarities and differences in productivity (whether material or symbolic) between the private and the public police. How might such differences affect macroeconomic trends in law enforcement? Moreover, Marx was interested in the fetishistic aspects of commodities – in our particular case, the commodity of security. Such analyses, however, have been rare and in dire need of empirical exemplars (see Spitzer, 1987; Loader, 1999). So far Marxian analysts of the police have not adequately considered how security is sold, how surplus value is extracted, how control of the workforce is maintained, and how security is symbolically produced and 'reproduced' dialectically. In sum, the need for a revived Marxian sensibility in our analyses of contract private security stems from the rather inane observation that these organizations are, after all, out to make a profit: they must *sell security*.[5] This has somehow escaped the attention of most contemporary theorists of the police. Late capitalism is about the relentless expansion of this epoch's mode of production into all facets of human endeavour (Jameson, 1984). Proprietors of contract security, as they themselves would gladly attest, do not perform their many functions, and firms do not innovate technologically to concoct even more extrusive measures, at the march of some unknown and mystic ethos of social control.

One of the central tasks I assigned myself at the outset of this research was to learn how private contract security functions as a profit-motivated business; put another way, to understand the parapolice as a part of broader social processes operating in a capitalist market society (Currie, 1997b). By extension, this meant shifting my thinking when it came to applying Marxian theory to policing, from state centrality to civil society and capital, which was, after all, the crux of Marx's voluminous writings and polymathematical thinking (Marx, 1970; 1972a; 1972b; 1973; 1976).[6] Marxist scholars have been critical of claims that the state uses its entitlement to force as a means for promoting a consensual 'greater good'; yet at the same time they sometimes unwittingly embrace (with liberal theorists) a myopic vision of policing by accepting without question that the state has a monopoly over policing (cf. Shearing, 1992) and thereby centring and privileging the state in their analyses. I do not contest that the state often acquiesces to bourgeois demands concerning the configuration of policing. I do, however, lament the lack of attention to the (very Marxian) idea that the development of these demands, and in part their satiation, happens outside the context of state perusal and intervention. The evolution of these policing demands has much less to do with the state per se than with the economic processes of late modern, capitalist, market society. Of course, these aspects of value, price, profit, commodity fetishism, and so on, need not be reserved for macroeconomic analyses; it is just as important to understand the 'micro-physics' of how contract private security is deployed if we are to make sense of how surplus-value is realized, and how contract security is represented, re-packaged, and sold as a commodity. Where Marxian theorists have been reluctant to tread, Foucauldian analysts employing the theoretically robust concepts of surveillance, discipline, and governmentality have been pioneering.

Foucauldian Approaches

In antithesis to conceptions of the state which assume its centrality in all social relations, including especially social control (e.g., Cohen, 1985; 1987), Foucauldian theorists argue for local, fragmented, conceptions of power that incorporate notions of discipline and surveillance (e.g., Burchell, Colin and Miller, 1991; Miller and Rose, 1995; Rose, 1996; Rose and Miller, 1992). This decentring of the state as an object of analysis when investigating power (Lowman, 1990) runs through most recent studies of neoliberalism and its effect on systems of discipline (O'Malley, 1992; 1993): 'By focusing primarily on the semi-autonomous relations of policing domestic security developed by private insurance companies, it has emerged quite clearly that the major processes of law enforcement are located in the nonstate field, and that these are formed in very significant ways independently of state initiatives for control' (O'Malley, 1991: 186).

Laissez-faire economics and the modes of governance that arise from it are linked to a retreat by the state (Garland, 1996) from its post-war proclivity to provide assistance to both citizenry and the market – a Keynesian logic (O'Malley and Palmer, 1996). As part of this retreat, sates turn responsibility over to citizens for providing the means for their own safety, security, and general well-being (Rose, 1996). In tandem with this, communities are made more and more responsible for solving their own crime problems. Thus, in opposition to what they rightly see as some of Marxist sociology's tendencies to reductionism and essentialism, pluralist theorists insist that governmental power has multiple objectives, and that the techniques applied to reach these objectives become differentiated as they are dispersed through locales largely beyond the state. They also argue that people relate to the exercise of governmental control as autonomous subjects and not as 'ideological dupes' (see Garland, 1997: 183, for a review).

In this tradition, Shearing and Stenning (1983) have proffered the best-known thesis on private policing, which focuses on the emergence of 'mass private property' holdings by large corporations. They argue that under the guise of privatization, the responsibility for maintaining peace is being transferred to corporate entities, and that peace is thereby being fundamentally redefined (Shearing and Stenning, 1983: 503). North America is experiencing a 'new feudalism,' wherein huge tracts of property – both private and public spaces – are now being controlled and policed by private corporate interests: 'These emerging conceptions conjure up an image of a world in which corporate "private governments" exist alongside state governments ... of shifting relations and claims with respect to sovereignty that change over both time and terrains' (Shearing, 1992: 425). Under such arrangements, policing is reconceptualized as a 'generic function' that cannot be understood as a monopoly of the state. The state is only one guarantor of order among many others. In this emerging redistribution of security, the state is no more relevant to the protection of property or people than the local 'government' of the corporation, or local community groups and tenants' associations that purchase security to augment guaranteed state-funded public policing.[7]

Accordingly, the analyst is encouraged to account for the local contingencies that facilitate or result in changes in police functions. This draws us to a series of questions that are best answered by utilizing more robust theoretical applications that are not tethered to universalizing notions of the state. The pluralist approach, however, has its limitations. Although it maintains that both the state and corporations are interchangeably important to the provision of security, and that their horizontal and autonomous natures are 'characterized by considerable fluidity and flux' (see also Henry, 1983; Shearing, 1993), it nonetheless adheres to a conceptual dichotomy between corporate and state security interests in earlier theorizing. Additionally, it does not consider alternative policing arrangements that aren't sponsored by either the state or large corporations. It has long and often been assumed that the goals of the public and private police are fundamentally different. The public police concern themselves with controlling crime and especially physical harm to people; the private police are tasked with preventing theft and property damage and with minimizing the likelihood of litigation against property owners. Thus, while the public police concern themselves with making 'good pinches' under their crime prevention mandate, the private police, under their 'loss prevention' mandate, drop 'snowflakes' (or notices of risks to property) in order to responsibilize workers (Shearing and Stenning, 1982b; 1983). This binary understanding of how security is organized elicits conclusions about the nature of private security that cannot account for its multiple manifestations. Of course, these same theorists are now beginning to realize that many private security companies *do* engage in crime control activities, whether in prisons, or in courts, or at public sites; in the same vein, many public police agencies are actively pursuing 'preventative' logics and employing business terminology to legitimize their activities and budgets (Kempa et al., 1999; Loader, 1999). Many policing services are now owned and managed by large corporations; but in addition to these, there are more complicated arrangements – for example, public housing corporations have hired private police officers under the direction of elected tenants' associations.[8] I contend that in this scenario, the private police (or parapolice) take on the responsibilities of crime control and become a *de facto* small municipal police service. When we divide up the deployment logics of policing services into public–private, crime prevention–loss prevention, and state–corporate, we can miss much of the diversity in modern policing arrangements.

Governmentality and Risk: A Marxist Critique

We must consider various other theoretical problems with the pluralist reaction to Marxian treatises on the police. Closely aligned with the 'mass private property' and 'loss prevention' approaches are the proponents of the Foucauldian concepts 'governmentality' and 'risk' (which are almost interchangeable in criminological terms). These approaches launch the most vociferous challenges to Marxism generally and to state-centred police theory specifically. In no small part, this is because Foucault himself was wary of universalizing notions, essentialist histories and 'fixed' or static conceptions of the social. In this sense, the challenges advanced by governmentality and risk theorists are a welcome and important reaction to some vulgar applications of Marxist thought. On the other hand, the anti-Marxian compulsion in the work of risk and governmentality theorists has meant that 'the baby has been thrown out with the bathwater.' Risk and governmentality theorists make indefensible claims about contingent history, the end of class, and the totality of surveillance mechanisms – claims that force us to question whether they are misapplying Foucauldian concepts and placing too much emphasis on nonmaterialist conceptions of social control (Rigakos and Hadden, 2001). Thus, both extant Marxian and Foucauldian theorists ignore economic motivations – the 'selling' of surveillance and the production of surplus-value – in the case of the Marxists because they have failed to appreciate Marx's core principles, and in the case of the Foucauldians because of a general anti-Marxian proclivity. In sum, there are many problems with the interwoven governmentality and risk perspectives as they relate to policing (see Rigakos, 1999, for a full critique). Below, I identify four limitations in the risk governance school that confound formulations of critical sociological problematics generally, and stunt our understanding of policing more specifically.

First and second, there are the political and philosophical limitations of *apoliticism* and *empirical agnosticism*, which in concert produce an environment for research that is theoretically limiting and ontologically mystifying to the police analyst. This is partly a result of divergent understandings and uses of Foucault's work on governmentality (1991a) and the archaeology of knowledge (1972), and partly a result of later claims-making about how Foucauldian methods and concepts are 'properly' to be implemented (O'Malley, 1996). This application of Foucault has resulted in a third important limitation, *historical myopia*, which privileges micro and contingent histories at the expense of long-term and durable accounts of risk and policing (Rigakos and Hadden, 2001) – accounts such as the emergence of the capitalist mode of production and, tied to it, the evolution of a 'projector' bourgeoisie. Risk theorists make claims about the structure of late modernity that are defensible only when this long-term history is ignored. Too much emphasis on variable and contingent history and a general anti-Marxian ethos produce empirically suspect (cf. Engel and Strasser, 1998), politically inadequate (Rustin, 1994; Leiss, 1994), and theoretically limiting claims that class has had its day as an object of investigation, as well as presumptions about 'new' postmodern risk categorizations. *Fourth*, recent neo-Weberian analyses employing risk society and governmentality orientations have promoted an understanding of professional organizations and institutions, including the police, that views front-line operatives as mere *automatons* who are enslaved by the risk information demands and protocols of the knowledge-producing structure. Policing agents are reduced to data collectors in the bureaucratic machinery, which is now understood as a risk-reducing and disciplining digital architecture of 'bio-power' (cf. Foucault, 1977; see Dandeker, 1990). Let us now examine these limitations, and their impact on police theorizing, in closer detail.

Perhaps, as proponents of governmentality studies (Burchell et al., 1991) maintain, Foucault cannot be criticized for neglecting to theorize about something he had no intention of examining in the first place. We might therefore accept the arguments of those Foucauldian scholars who argue that the 'social' has limits (Rose and Miller, 1996), and who see Foucault's work as empirically agnostic (O'Malley, Weir and Shearing, 1997; O'Malley, 2001) about ideas such as class and 'real' risk – in other words, who view Foucault's project as quite separate from general sociological problematics, histories and investigations of social phenomena and social problems. In carving out space for the 'doing' of governmentality in criminology, O'Malley and colleagues (1997: 502) argue that Foucauldian genealogical work is epistemologically different from the more familiar historical and sociological approach of examining rule by observing and documenting 'what *actually* happened.' Elsewhere, O'Malley (2001) creates a sharp distinction between, on the one hand, the type of work he and other 'risk' governmentality theorists are engaged in and, on the other hand, the work of risk theorists like Ulrich Beck (1992b) and Ericson and Haggerty (1997). Beck and Ericson and Haggerty are concerned with 'real risks'; in contrast, O'Malley sees such ontological risks – or any pronouncement about the *actual* conditions of postmodernity – as extraneous to Foucault's project. Approached this way, techniques of governance – these schemes of social order – can be treated separately from the mapping of fears, insecurities, and actual changes in risk conditions. Of course, this need not be the case: this is only *one* approach to Foucault – and a rather dubious one.

This idea of focusing solely on paper realities, 'system imaginaries' (Bogard, 1996), or schemas and programs (Foucault, 1991a) – in other words, bypassing any responsibility for analysing the 'social' – stems from a particular reading of Foucault. When asked how the Benthamite prisoner might negotiate his reality or resist the intrusive surveillance described in *Discipline and Punish*, Foucault replied, 'you see that this has nothing to do with the project – an admirable one in itself – of grasping a "whole society" in its "living reality"' (Foucault, 1991b: 181). Foucault was indicating here that he cared less about the general socio-logical problem of analysing social relations per se, than he did about understanding institutional schemas as mechanisms by which discipline is imagined. For Foucault, however, this was not a statement of empiri-cal privilege, nor was it a template for the *proper* way to conduct research:

> If I had wanted to describe 'real life' in the prisons, I wouldn't have indeed gone to Bentham. But the fact that this real life isn't the same as the theo-retician's schemas doesn't entail that these schemas are therefore utopian, imaginary, etc. One could only think that if one had a very impoverished notion of the real. For one thing, the elaboration of these schemas corre-sponds to a whole series of diverse practices and strategies ... For another thing, *these programmes induce a whole series of effects in the real (which isn't of course the same as saying they take the place of the real):* they crystallize into insti-tutions, they inform individual behaviour, they act as grids for the percep-tion and evaluation of things. (Foucault, 1991b: 81; author's emphasis).

Foucault is saying two very important things here. *First*, he is conceding that there are in fact differences between the institutional 'reality' he is demystifying and analysing – the control logics of the prison – and the reality of 'prison *life*.' The former, he accepts, cannot act as a replace-ment for the latter. *Second*, he is arguing that although these schemas are not 'real' in and of themselves, even so they produce a broad range of responses that are *very real in their consequences*: they inform behaviour, perception, and resistance. Here, Foucault is telling us that a dialectic relationship is possible between programmatic schemas and the people who are ostensibly ensnared by them – they are equally relevant, and equally important for us to understand the system. For example, the presence of even more security measures may often produce even more insecurity (cf. Spitzer, 1987) and myriad forms of resistance.

Associated with ontological pronouncements about which forms of risk are worth investigating are strangely naïve assertions about the 'political neutrality' of governmentality discourses. It may be possible to delimit the political nature and implications of a project if you have already disavowed its involvement with 'what actually happened.' Where there is no truth claim, there is no political claim – or so it would seem. But this little bit of mental gymnastics is antithetical to critical sociology. After reviewing the governmentality literature for its applicability to criminology and sociology, Garland (1997: 186) noted that 'this approach will tend to imply a critical stance – insofar as it is describing modes of exercising power ... it seeks to maintain the neutral gaze of an analyst rather than the hostile glare of a rival with competing truth claims.' Garland finds this 'valuable.' Of course, it was long ago demonstrated that it is impossible for criminologists to avoid being politically implicated on their own analyses (Becker, 1967). This makes Garland's lament for a critical reading of penal practices rather bewildering – but only because he accepts the premise that governmentality might very well be politically neutral: 'But alongside this knowledge of the authorities' knowledge, I also want to be able to propose a different reading of what causes crime, why controls are failing, why penal-warfare measures no longer seem adequate' (1997: 201). And here Garland realizes that this alternative account will surely encompass 'the dynamics of the social field, or the life-world to be governed' (1997: 201). Nowhere can we see more clearly the ontological mystification and perceived political disengagement of governmentality linked (and confounded) than in Garland's irked appraisal. But of course, the point here is that neither Garland, nor anyone else, need bemoan the political limits of risk theory and the critical use of Foucault, since these limits are in the first instance fabricated and in the second unnecessary. The upshot of this retrenchment – this devolution of Foucauldian methods and the very cautious application of governmentality to criminology – is that some genealogies of risk become myopic, that is, fragmented into micro-histories and oblivious to long-term, durable *lignes de conduit.* This is in no small part due to a stubborn insistence on ignoring the 'social' (Rose and Miller, 1992) and the reality of risk (O'Malley 2001). Realist conceptions of science and history are thus tossed aside, and with them, Marx and political economy.

The cost to a cogent and coherent history of risk is regrettable. If we resign ourselves to understanding risk society as post-Keynesian (O'Malley and Palmer, 1996), prudentialist (O'Malley and others) and somehow intrinsically late (Ericson and Haggerty, 1997) or postmodern, we cannot then see risk ideology for what it really is – a discourse well entrenched in bourgeois thought and rooted in the plans of seventeenth-century

English 'projectors' (insurance schemers) and the rise of capitalism (Rigakos and Hadden, 2001). Once we unwisely resolve that 'risk is new,' all actuarial thought and all categorizations and constructions of risk identities may be seen as ushering in a new era of penology (Feeley and Simon, 1994), the death of class (Beck, 1992b; Ericson and Haggerty, 1997), and the end of economics as we know it (O'Malley, 2001).

As we have seen, some risk theorists have read Foucault in such a way as to cast him as a relativist, an empirical agnostic, and by extension as sometimes an apolitical thinker. Clearly, submersion in the logics of an institution's techniques of social control often results in an unfettered acceptance of risk schemas as 'total' or complete (a limitation shared with certain Marxist accounts). This misrepresents the realities of those populations meant to be ensnared by the system. In short order, the members of those populations are reduced to mere automatons. In his treatment of medical doctors Castel argues that the 'essential component of intervention no longer takes the form of direct face-to-face relationships between the carer and the cared' (1991: 281). Instead, intervention resides in the 'establishing of *flows of population*' based on a range of factors that indicate risk. For Castel, this means that 'the specialists find themselves now cast in a subordinate role, while managerial policy formation is allowed to develop into a completely autonomous force, totally beyond the surveillance operative on the ground who is now reduced to mere executant' (1991: 281).

Ericson and Haggerty (1997) note this same dynamic in their treatment of risk systems operating in Canada's public police. In their analysis they privilege auditing systems, report formats, and the hierarchy of communications, and reimagine street-level officers as field workers checking off boxes in a prescribed, non-narrative reporting system. Police officers are seen as deskilled and as having limited decision-making options, all of which must fall within the policies and procedures established by professional senior officers and policymakers. (Ericson is arguing here against his own work [1982], in which he sees police subcultural 'recipe rules' and occupational mores as important determinants of actions and mobilization.) Yet even in Ericson and Haggerty's study we find many examples of police officers resisting these deskilling systems, for example, by circulating bootleg report forms, misusing information technology, and refusing to work with computers. These games of resistance demonstrate the existence of a dialectic of control, however much the authors try to emphasize the managerial regimen (see also Manning, 1992; 1996).

Bogard (1996) is far more daring than Ericson and Haggerty (1997) in his treatment of hypercontrol in telematic societies (see Rigakos, 1998). In his social science *fiction* project, he argues that 'a picture emerges of an "observation machine" that fashions its own images for its own consumption' (1996: 24), and that leaves nothing to chance and accounts for everything from the very beginning. The police officer of the future lets the computer scan information on the network for profile anomalies, and then selects targets, who are immediately arrested: 'Direct, "hands-on" surveillance, if you will, is bypassed or short-circuited: it's already done, or at least on automatic. Having to watch or wait for an infraction is a thing of the past, if you're a police officer' (1996: 54). To be fair, Bogard's exercise is a study of a *system imaginary*; none of these trends actually exist in their ideal today. In Bogard's understanding of telematic society, labour (cyborgwork) is allowed leisure time, but only because this ultimately feeds back into the totalizing system of surveillance production. In other words, even loafing is actuarially precoded to elicit maximum profit. Nothing, then, escapes the monolithic march of the machine: every action and reaction has already been accounted for (read: actuarially predicted) and serves only to feed back into the improvement of the system. So in many ways, the 'alternative' thinking of poststructural approaches merely replaces one totalizing set of notions about the social world with another when it comes to formal control, private policing, and, by extension, contract private security.

Parapolicing Risk Markets

I use the term 'risk markets' in this book because I want to distinguish my model from the 'risk society' model, which denies any role to class, and because I want to differentiate my approach from risk thinking in governmentality circles, where notions of economy are eschewed altogether. This is not the place to repeat my general polemics against such discourses (see Rigakos, 1999; Rigakos and Hadden, 2001), suffice it to say that these orientations rely on a particular reading of Foucault that limits his insights to non-sociological problematics, and on an unwarranted rejection of Marx – two formulations (among others) that I reject. In this book I am not offering a new 'theory' of private police, nor am I making a revolutionary break with previous thinking on private policing. My goal is far more modest: to draw attention to some fundamental aspects of contract private security previously unattended to in criminological theorizing. Though I have reservations about Foucauldian and Marxian formulations, it is quite clear that the most thoughtful and groundbreaking work on private policing has taken place within their scope.

The object of my analysis is a contract private security firm called Intelligarde International. As I noted in the introduction, the Intelligarde parapolice provide an important opportunity to test extant theory. They constitute an almost perfect exemplar of risk, actuarialism, and loss prevention, as well as a confounding exception to these often overstated governmental logics. I am using Intelligarde as a case study for a risk markets approach, and have borrowed the term 'parapolice' directly from that organization. The parapolice are only 'new' insofar as they have recently (and purportedly) revolutionized the contract private security industry in Canada by taking on functions similar to those of the public municipal police. The company's managers contend that they accept risky contracts, have far more professional guards, look, act, and train like 'law enforcement professionals,' and so on. Anecdotal evidence suggests that the parapolice have spawned 'copy-cat' competitors. Even larger Toronto contract security firms (such as Intercon) have being trying to emulate them.

I do not claim that Intelligarde is a typical company in the private contract security industry in Canada, or even in Toronto. Intelligarde's parapolice are *not* the industry standard. Even so, the postulates I advance in the chapters that follow should not be confined to the parapolice, since they are based on more *general* theories of private policing. The fact that Intelligarde is exceptional may lead us to modify our theories of private policing – specifically, it may lead us to include this type of security organization in future theoretical formulations. This is especially true if it is later shown that the parapolice are harbingers of a new (relatively speaking) movement in private contract security. A risk markets orientation may or may not be applicable to other private policing contexts, not because it is a limited approach that seeks to make sense of only one particular form of contract private security, but rather because it is a general orientation based on existing theories that may or may not have other significant exemplars. I leave this empirical question to subsequent researchers.

The most obvious need for a reorientation in theory stems from the fact that police theorists have rarely made the banal observation that contract private security is a profit-making enterprise. It is my contention that this simple fact requires us to carefully revisit Marxian analyses, especially as they relate to political economy. However, this study, does not deal with these issues at the macro-sociological level – that is, it does not consider the role of inequality and its relationship to bourgeois fortification; nor does it consider the relationship between the growth in private policing and changes in the political economy and commodification; nor the rate of extraction of surplus-value from contract security personnel; nor the transnational quality of monstrous security conglomerates that serve to finally and completely alienate citizens from their own means of security; nor the ultimate triumph of the alienation of 'safety' in both its material and its ephemeral, immaterial forms. This project does consider how social control is commodified, specifically in the context of the services that Intelligarde sells. In simplest terms, commodification refers to the incessant expansion of capital and, by extension, the transformation of aspects of human existence into a commodified form. In other words, it explains how people come to measure tangible and intangible human activities and products not by their use-value but rather by their exchange-value: 'A thing can be useful, and a product of human labour, without being a commodity. He who satisfies his own need with the product of his own labour admittedly creates use-values, but no commodities' (Marx, 1976: 131). In this context, security was once a general activity of citizens, and later a service expensed against state or private revenues, and has now become something to be contracted privately. Put another way, it once had only use-value, and then had exchange-value added to it, and has now become something from which capitalists can extract surplus-value. To summarize this chapter, and thus to rearticulate the postulates guiding this research, I can say the following:

1. The modern institutional response to risk relies heavily on the production of knowledge about 'dangerous' populations. This knowledge is based on actuarial practices, and seeks to make risky populations known through the disciplining practices of surveillance. Although these techniques seem to depoliticize the construction of suitable enemies by erecting rationalistic and economic decision-making templates, they nonetheless reproduce the same disparities.
2. Actuarial practices come to define both internal and external risk categorizations for both organizational staff and the populations being policed. These managerial techniques provide insight into the operational logics of an institution, but do not explain the multiple

modes of resistance, or the subcultural logics of the policers and policed. For almost every disciplinary schema, there exists a correlative mode of resistance in a dialectic of control.

3. In modern times security provision is not typically organized around the state. Multiple private arrangements operate under corporate and other local controls that defy artificial dichotomous formulations such as public–private, crime prevention–loss prevention, and state–corporate constructs.

4. The nature of security provision in late modernity is characterized by the selling of commodified social control to risk markets that have been created by fear. This process is amplified by late capitalist production logics and by the continued consumerization of citizens.

5. Contract security labour is alienated labour on multiple levels. It must be presented as 'quantifiable' in order for the security worker to become a literal money-making 'apparatus' of surveillance. This creates further insecurity and alienation between citizens.

6. Private security must be understood in the context of its existence, as a profit-making enterprise under the capitalist mode of production.

The next chapter explains the methodology I employed to operationalize this investigative framework.

TWO

Methods of Inquiry

In the previous chapter I outlined a theoretical framework for this project that seeks to bridge gaps in previous research while also asking new questions about the parapolice. This investigation extends the scholarship of risk and governmentality discourses while emphasizing the role of Marxian conceptions of commodity fetishism and political economy. As Wagner (1984) has pointed out, behind each set of research question, there exists a sometimes explicit, sometimes implicit orienting strategy. In this book I carry the postulates itemized in the preceding chapter into a case study of the Intelligarde parapolice. There are two central research questions emanating from this model and driving this project:

1. How is discipline and surveillance achieved organizationally and sold externally to risk markets?
2. How do security agents and those they are tasked with policing resist social control?

These questions require the researcher to describe first, how commodified security is marketed and provided, and second, how this process is resisted by the populations meant to be policed as well as by those doing the policing.

In the summer of 1997 I conducted research on the private security industry in the Greater Toronto Area (GTA). The point of the project was to query selected security executives about the privatization of policing and the overlapping functions of the public and private police. In the course of that study I came upon Intelligarde International, a contract private security firm that is actively extending private policing into the public domain. During data collection I was constantly being directed to Intelligarde by competing security executives, who often referred derisively to their 'breaking the law' or 'trying to be cops.' After meeting with Intelligarde's president and owner Ross McLeod, it became obvious to me that if the sociology of policing was to get serious about 'commodification,' 'privatization,' 'risk management,' and the new parapolice in Canada, it would have to start with his company.

With the Canadian public growing more and more uneasy about safety and security provision, both public and private (see International Crime Victimization Survey, 1992), Intelligarde International has begun to receive considerable media attention. While I was conducting my research, Intelligarde was featured in Canada's national newsmagazine *Maclean's* (Palango, 1998) and on the Canadian Broadcasting Corporation's *Witness* program (23 January 1998). The company is a $6 million business. It has been operating for sixteen years, mainly in the GTA, although it may soon have a presence in small communities across Ontario. Intelligarde is almost unique in that it requires its security officers to make arrests and takes on parapolicing functions such as clearing crack houses, processing evictions, and even disrupting the business of 'drug gangs.'

I arranged to conduct this research project in late August of 1997, but did not begin collecting data until mid-September. The methods I employed reflected the overall objectives of this book. That is, I employed multiple investigative approaches reflecting this study's dual (i.e., discriptive and theoretical) mandate.[1] There are seven sources of data for this book: ethnography, formal interviews, the occurrence database, personnel files, the banning database, Intelligarde communications and internal documents, and media representations of Intelligarde (including a search of the *Toronto Star* database).[2] In this chapter I consider each method in turn, including why I used it, and the actual process of data collection.

Critical Ethnography

Lofland has argued that 'in order to "do" qualitative field research, one needs only himself [or herself], time, some people to watch and/or talk to, and writing materials. It is organizationally and technologically the most individualized and primitive of research genres' (1974: 111). Yet as I have already noted, critical ethnography involves more than simple observation. Critical researchers begin from the tenet that all cultural (and subcultural) life is in a constant state of tension between control and resistance (Thomas, 1993: 9); they expose even mundane events for their broader social processes of coercion, evasion, control, and reform. These tensions are to be found in the rituals, behaviours, sustaining narratives, communications systems, and general mores of a given culture. Because ethnographic analyses of the private police are completely absent from the published literatures, many questions about the everyday routines of private security officers have not been answered. This absence is especially striking when we consider how many ethnographic analyses of the public police have been conducted, and how old some of them are (e.g., Skolnick, 1966; Westley, 1970). More important from a risk markets perspective is that in the absence of an ethnography of parapolicing, we cannot answer the empirical questions posited earlier. Until we immerse ourselves in the daily practices of maintaining surveillance and managing risks, the nuances of selling commodified social control must remain unanalysed.

Recent work on the police has brought to the surface intellectual schisms between early subcultural investigations (e.g., Ericson, 1982; Manning and Van Maanen, 1978; Skolnick, 1966; Smith and Gray, 1983) and modern analyses of 'governance' (e.g., Dandeker, 1990; Ericson and Haggerty, 1997; Ericson, Haggerty and Carriere, 1993). In contrast to these studies, a critical ethnography of risk markets does not separate control from resistance, systems from persons, or governance from agency. Exposing the dialectic nature of these relationships is central to the ethnographic enterprise (cf. Goffman, 1961). A risk markets perspective employs critical ethnography to unravel the processes by which discipline, surveillance, and resistance are negotiated. In this sense, critical ethnography links the microsociological practices of private policing to the macrosociological political processes of risk markets. The mundane procedures of private law enforcement and surveillance as products of neoliberal actuarial logics are thereby revealed for their commodified nature. If Intelligarde security officers engage in crime control, this will become evident during the ethnography. So when investigating the (private) policing of 'risk markets,' we must understand how the Intelligarde parapolice have been affected by the development of current practices. How is surveillance and discipline imagined, and how is it resisted, by those within and outside the organization? Linked to this, how is Intelligarde's social control capability sold as a commodity to private clients, tenants' associations, and police boards?

In the next section I describe how I went about conducting formal field interviews with an assortment of respondents both within and outside the organization. The primary aim of the interviews was to gain an understanding of the goals, fears, and desires of the respondents; however, field observations sometimes yielded better data about these issues. On tape, security officers tended to be reserved. They were often much more forthcoming when they gathered in groups, as they often did; on these occasions the banter, storytelling, and general gossip were fascinating. These gatherings were typically held in the briefing room, in front of the duty desk, in the car bays (when the supervisor was absent), or at selected sites in the downtown area. It immediately became apparent to me that certain 'war stories' had spread quickly through the ranks and achieved the status of subcultural lore. I would hear them over and over from both veterans and rookies. I make reference to these stories throughout the book.

I began my feld observations in September 1997 and continued them until early November. I spent most of my time with either mobile or static officers. Sometimes I rode along with mobile patrol officers as they attended 'hits,'[3] alarm responses, or backed up fellow officers. Other times I rode in a vehicle patrolling an adjacent district, or I asked to be dropped off at various sites to interview static officers. I conducted formal interviews with one-quarter of the uniformed officers, but I actually spoke to and noted the comments of many more than that: including field notes and interviews, I recorded contacts with roughly half of Intelligarde's staff.[4] The ethnographic fieldwork produced 350 pages of notes[5] and roughly 126 hours of observational data. Daily field observations lasted between one and fourteen hours. In the following chapters, I provide observations in narrative format. Mixed in with recorded discussions and other occurrences are my own subjective interpretations. The observer's placement in relation to the data is of vital importance in critical ethnography (Thomas, 1993), so I provide data on my movements and speech relative to the activities around me. The direct observation of parapolicing provided me with insights into the processes of surveillance and commodification.

Formal Interviews

The purpose of the formal interviews was to gain insight into the commodified nature of security provision in risk markets. In the interviews I focused on how surveillance and resistance are negotiated by examining

TABLE 2.1
Formal interviews conducted

Personnel	Male N	%	Female N	%	Visible others N	%
Mobile security officer (N = 14)	12	85.7	2	14.3	3	21.4
Static security officer (N = 17)	14	82.3	3	17.6	6	35.3
Communications officer (N = 4)	4	100	0	0	0	0
Intelligarde management (N = 5)	5	100	0	0	0	0
GTA Security executives (N = 10)	10	100	0	0	0	0

the attitudes of both managers and line officers. Through these interviews, candid information about the logics of company mobilizations came to light that no amount of paper chasing would have revealed. In these interviews I also sought to establish the mission of parapolicing as crime fighting within a 'wannabe' culture; in this way I was reversing a tendency of previous research, which focuses on the attitudes of corporate managers (Shearing, Stenning, and Addario, 1985a), the public police (Shearing, Stenning, and Addario, 1985b) or the general public (Shearing, Stenning, and Addario, 1985c).[6] I was asking, the parapolice for their own perceptions of outside agents.

I conducted fifty interviews for this book. Ten were with security executives and a former president of the Independent Professional Alarm Dealers association; these had formed the basis of an earlier investigation (see Beare and Rigakos, 1997: 1).[7] These interviews were designed to test the attitudes of select security executives about the history, growth, and future direction of private policing. Because the interviews questions were open-ended and specific to the company at hand, these interviews almost always deviated considerably from the schedule.[8] I conducted a further forty interviews with Intelligarde staff, ranging in rank from president to security officer. Different questions were posed to Intelligarde's field staff, to managers, and to other security executives. The interview schedule addressed these issues: the work, the company, media coverage of Intelligarde, training, career aspirations, contact with the public police, and whatever additional issues that arose the interviews. Managers were asked about the organization's direction, history, and mobilizations. Job-specific queries were also made.

Table 2.1 indicates whom I interviewed for this study. At the time of research, the company employed 141 uniformed security personnel:[9] 35

(24.8 per cent) were assigned to mobile patrol, 92 (65.2 per cent) to static sites, and 6 (4.3 per cent) to both functions. Another 6 (4.3 per cent) worked in dispatch as communications officers. I tried to interview an equal number of mobile and static security officers because I had grounds to believe there were differences in subcultural mores between the two groups. This was reflected in the claims made by each group regarding the difficulty, excitement, and rewards of various postings.[10] There is also evidence that mobile assignments have higher status than static ones – Intelligarde staff often note that it is a 'privilege' to work in motorized patrol. I made particular effort to oversample members of visible minority populations and women. Of the 11 women employed by Intelligarde for uniform duties, I interviewed 5 (45 per cent). Similarly, I spoke to nine (28 per cent) of the company's 32 visible minority members. In total, then, I conducted formal interviews with 35 (24.8 per cent) uniform personnel and 5 (71 per cent) of the 7 managers and office staff. Many of Intelligarde's employees perform multiple functions, and this makes it difficult to categorize their activities. This is especially true of personnel listed as both mobile and static site officers. Most of Intelligarde's managers are licensed security guards and wear uniforms while doing office work. The quality control manager spent a considerable amount of his shift in the office, but at times engaged in patrol and investigative functions, sometimes alongside the operations manager, who exchanged his suit for a uniform while on patrol.

To obtain interviews, I approached security officers and presented them with a letter of permission signed by Intelligarde's sales and marketing director. Then, I asked them if they would let me interview them. I often conducted interviews in the course of ethnographic observation. Typically, this involved in-car or on-site interviews while the mobile or static officer was on patrol. I conducted other interviews at the station while analysing electronic databases, or immediately after briefings. Only two security officers refused initially to be interviewed. In both cases, however, they later approached me and agreed to answer questions. In the first instance, the security officer was kilometres away from his assigned property and did not want to be recorded astray from his post. In the second, the security officer was too busy at the time to talk but sought me out when our paths crossed two weeks later. Most of Intelligarde's security officers were at first suspicious of me, just as the public police would have been (e.g., Ericson, 1982; Manning, 1997; Rigakos, 1995; Skolnick, 1966). However, they gradually accepted the research project.[11] Some officers were convinced that I was a spy for the company president, Ross McLeod, and I had to reassure them I wasn't. Some security officers asked me to pass messages to management regarding working conditions and morale, under guarantees of anonymity.

Most of the interviews (45 of 50 = 90 per cent) were recorded on audiotape, but a few respondents asked me to take notes instead. On two other occasions I ran out of audiotape. In total, I recorded over eleven hours of interviews that were eventually transcribed. The interviews lasted between fifteen minutes and one hour. I destroyed the original tapes after transcribing them, in accordance with ethics requirements concerning the confidentiality of respondents' answers. There are no identifiers on the transcripts except for the officer's rank, ethnicity, and sex. To maintain a degree of anonymity, I will refer to office or managerial staff as 'Intelligarde managers' when I quote them in this book. These formal interviews lend the data greater structure and consistency.

Occurrence, Personnel, and Bannings Databases

Occurrence reports relay important information in narrative form to Intelligarde management and clientele. This makes them vitally important for understanding the company's mobilizations. The modern institutional response to threats is wedded to the production of knowledge about 'dangerous' populations. The occurrence reports can help test whether the parapolice of Intelligarde are indeed engaged in crime control activities; this in turn provides triangulative data to support or challenge ethnographic observations. The data gathered from the occurrence reports also fulfil a descriptive mandate, in that statistical information on parapolicing mobilizations has not previously been available.

These documents differ from patrol reports: they communicate 'incidents' considered special or out of the ordinary. Unfortunately, there is no specific protocol for line officers regarding when an occurrence report should be produced. Often, less important matters such as resident queries and noise complaints are routinely filed as occurrences at one site, but not at another. These variations often reflect client demands – itself an example of the commodification of information. They also often reflect the inexperience of newer security officers, who it is said are more likely to produce paperwork in hopes of looking busy and impressing managers. Whenever police or outside agencies were involved or arrests were made, Intelligarde security officers invariably filed occurrence reports. This was for litigation purposes and, as one respondent put it, for the sake of 'C.Y.A. man – cover your ass.'

Intelligarde files all occurrence reports completed by security officers. Most of the more recent reports were considered 'hot' and so had not yet been filed. So as not to interfere with the company's immediate operations, I restricted my research to 'cold' files from the one-year period preceding my research: September 1996 to August 1997. These files were archived by month submitted and by site, along with routine site reports (e.g., mobile inspection reports). I had to separate the occurrence reports from their folders, code them, and input them to an SPSS data file. The variables I constructed from the occurrence files included:

- the type of occurrence
- the badge number of the security officer filing the report,
- whether police, ambulatory, fire, or other services were called,
- the number of security officers involved,
- whether a weapon was used, and its type,
- the outcome or result of intervention, *and*
- whether injuries resulted, and to whom.

A total of 1,703 occurrence reports had been filed at Intelligarde headquarters between September 1996 and August 1997. A systematic random sample[12] of these yielded 340 reports for coding, data entry, and analysis. This resulted in a margin of error at the 95 per cent confidence interval of ±5 per cent ($p = .05$).

Who are these private cops? Where do they come from? What experience do they have? What education do they come equipped with? If we are to begin answering these questions, we have to know about the demographic particulars of Intelligarde's staff. Access to the company's personnel files was granted by the president, marketing director, and general manager after consultation with the director of human resources. I coded a total of 141 files and input them into an SPSS database. Sixteen files represented Intelligarde employees securing an Ottawa shopping mall (a 'satellite site'); I did not include these in the sample population. I omitted another 34 files from the personnel database because these employees were no longer with the company. The main source of personal information in the staff files was the employee's application for a security guard and/or private investigator licence. These forms included the applicant's date of birth, country of birth, residence, criminal record, complexion, height, and weight, along with other optional particulars such as education and past employment as a security guard. The company's own application forms[13] offered additional information. A final source of information was the applicant's résumé, which typically included training information and previous security, police, or military experience. Unfortunately, some files were incomplete, and because of the company's privacy policies I was not permitted to contact Intelligarde personnel by telephone to complete the dossiers. In any case, I coded the file information onto 'Intelligarde Security Officer Personnel Summary Sheets,' which included the employee's name, licence information, residence, previous employment, citizenship, height, weight, complexion, education, offences, and training with the company. After preparing the summary sheets, I turned them over to Intelligarde's chief scheduling officer, who indicated whether the employee was working in mobile patrol or at a site, and what duty the security officer was qualified to undertake.

Intelligarde's 'banning' database is integral to its daily operations, and is the main source of information about individuals issued an NPE (notice prohibiting entry) on properties secured by the company. The police produce information about risky populations in response to institutional demands for safety. In this regard, the NPE database is central to Intelligarde's operations and to the maintenance of its risk markets. An organization's ability to amass information about dangerous populations that its agents come into contact with is a commodified ingredient of modern policing arrangements; at the same time it helps guide appropriate police actions in the future. The construction of 'persons known to the police' does a great deal to determine subsequent police–citizen interactions. To answer the question posed earlier – How is discipline and surveillance achieved? – we must analyse the information by which an organization comes to 'know' the populations under its purview. I did not construct the bannings database; it already existed in electronic form, and had for a number of years. To construct a one-year sample, I selected all entries between August 1996 and September 1997.[14] I then had the database scanned and translated into SPSS format; in the process, thousands of string variables were converted into numeric codes. Although the database served Intelligarde's communications needs, it could not be used for statistical analysis without significant manipulation. Surveillance variables that appeared on the NPEs, such as the banned individual's hair length, height, weight, clothing style, eyewear, and markings or tattoos, were omitted from analysis. Significant recoding was required for all other variables, including sex, location, complexion, age, address, and the reasons for banning.

In total, I gleaned 2,617 cases for statistical analysis from the Intelligarde banning database; this represented one year of mobilizations by Intelligarde security officers. This raw frequency alone demonstrates how well Intelligarde carries out its social control function.[15] In this book, I refer repeatedly to data from this information source.

Communications and Other Internal Documents

Like other policing organizations, Intelligarde spends an enormous amount of time collecting and disseminating information (Ericson and Haggerty, 1997; Ericson, Haggerty, and Carriere, 1993). The resulting materials provide tremendous insight into the workings of the company and reveal its vision, goals, and marketing techniques. To sell parapolicing, Intelligarde must provide both public and private clients with evidence of a tangible security product. All of the report writing serves multiple purposes; most importantly, however, it serves to monitor both staff and public and to minimize liability. There are over a dozen report forms to fill out, including tag tow reports, parking tickets, weekly time sheets, evidentiary cover reports, occurrence reports, alarm reports, alarm response reports, 30 minute plus alarm response forms, NPEs, equipment and key sign sheets, mobile inspection reports, checklists for fire-related incidents, run sheets (including 'non-revenue' items), vehicle inspection sheets, officer k-9 reports, and roll call. In addition to these, I utilized internal memorandums ($n = 10$), training materials, and letters or faxes into or out of the company ($n = 5$) in order to understand the mobilizations and organizational logics of Intelligarde. The report formats, training literatures, and communications amount to over 300 pages of information.

The Media

A final area of investigation is the media's depictions of Intelligarde. This is important from the perspective of amassing information about the company's reputation among journalists and the general public, and also because it affects the self-perceptions of Intelligarde security officers. Police officers often assess job fulfilment and 'good pinches' in relation to cinema and media portrayals of police work (Mallett, 1996). We also know that the dramaturgical nature of police representation depends heavily on public presentations and the symbol and meanings attached to them (Manning, 1997). The parapolice are no different.

Recent stories in the media about Intelligarde coincided with the period of data collection, and included both print and television stories. In Toronto the print media have long been curious about Intelligarde's operations, and this has resulted in wildly different, but mostly simplistic, accounts of what Intelligarde does. These stories have a strong effect on private policing, in the sense that Intelligarde security officers regularly refer to media depictions of them as a basis for discussing other issues. It is quite common for a 'misunderstood' social group to rally against 'misplaced' vilifications or around positive and reaffirming portrayals, so it is important to map these tendencies and their effects on Intelligarde personnel.

I have now outlined the theoretical orientation and the methods of analysis for this study. In the next chapter I place the new parapolice in context.

THREE

The New Parapolice

As one enters Terminal 3 at Toronto's Pearson International Airport, one notices the newness of the structures, the cleanliness of the walls and ceilings, and the brightness and bustle of the building. Passengers move along various cues for airline tickets, baggage checks, and car rentals. Perhaps less noticeable are two of Canada's federal police talking to a pair of constables from the Peel Regional Police Service. After the discussion ends, the RCMP officers begin to patrol, nodding hello to two security officers from Excalibur Security making similar rounds. Farther along, they watch two armed Brinks guards carry money satchels from a nearby currency exchange kiosk. They wind by Commissionaires issuing parking tickets and Group 4 Securitas security guards checking the luggage of passengers. On the lower level, Canada Customs agents spot a suspicious traveller and call for the RCMP and an immigration officer. In a processing centre just off the tarmac, security guards from Metropol Security meet with the immigration officials while the detainee is handed over to the security firm for transport to the privately run Mississauga Immigration Detention Centre (MIDC). The detainee is handcuffed, placed in the caged rear of an unmarked van, and driven to the centre, which from the outside looks like just another inconspicuous motel. As one gets closer, however, one sees a 12-foot chain link fence topped with barbed wire encircling the rear of the building.

Just an unremarkable tour of Canada's busiest airport?[1] Perhaps, but on this short imaginary stroll you have come under the gaze of three federal policing agencies, one municipal police service, a quasi-public security force, four privately contracted security companies, and an unknown number of in-house airline security agencies, all of them working alongside one another in a generally smooth-running chain of surveillance. This is how people and property are secured in late capitalist risk markets. The RCMP has taken on the policing contract at the airport but works alongside the local police in conducting investigations and distributing information about offenders and various threats. As part of the contract, the RCMP has hired a private security firm to undertake some of the more monotonous policing functions. Similarly, it has hired the Corps of Commissionaires to issue parking tickets. The baggage inspection contract was tendered, and won by the security multinational Group 4 Securitas. The Department of Immigration has contracted out the MIDC and detainee transport to Metropol Security. There are myriad threats to social order in any airport, and this creates myriad opportunities for selling, trading, and contracting security provision. Not all security providers are for-profit firms, but they are all governed by the same market logics: they hold on to their clients by providing a service for a fee that is competitive. In the United States, because of the growth in civil litigation (Priest, 1990), institutions have been taking steps to minimize their liability by enforcing regulations in certain spaces. Enforcement requires surveillance as well as agents to point out and react to violations. In their efforts to minimize liability, social institutions are relying more and more on private security agents and technologies.

It is worthwhile to investigate specific sites of security provision, but we could just as profitably examine the security organizations themselves. For example, in the case of the Toronto airport scenario we may decide to more closely scrutinize Group 4 Securitas. We would note that this transnational corporation has security offices in twenty-nine countries, including Canada. Also, that it owns security technology companies in eleven countries and runs private correctional services in the United States, England, and Australia. And finally, that its operations are spreading quickly – it has recently signed contracts to police New Zealand's parklands and to run a large part of South Australia's correctional and prisoner transport services (Stemman, 1997). So it is quite possible to watch Securitas guards run our carry-on luggage through the metal detectors at Toronto's airport and later, having landed in Australia, watch Securitas guards check our luggage again. Were we then to visit a South Australian mall or condominium, we might well again find ourselves under the watchful gaze of Securitas. Were we then, for argument's sake, caught shoplifting, a Securitas guard would arrest us and turn us over to the police. Where we then to appear in court, we might well find a guard in a Securitas uniform providing security. Were we detained for something more serious, chances are that a Securitas guard would be patrolling outside our cell. Were we found guilty and sentenced to jail, we would be transported in a prisoner van owned and operated by Securitas to a Securitas-run private jail such as Mount Gambier or the Metropolitan Men's Prison. All of this makes most people nervous, for various reasons: security is becoming more multinational, and this raises questions about the legitimacy and accountability of governments. There are also more mundane concerns – for example, how competent are the people who staff these organizations? How well trained? What motivates them? Multinational security corporations such as Wackenhut, Burns, and Pinkerton's are making our trip through Securitas's security network less and less unusual. Since the Second World War, private security firms have slowly been taking over public policing functions, and this is forcing us to ask some rather important questions about the conceptual division of 'public' and 'private.' Does this dichotomy disguise more than it reveals about policing?

In this chapter I establish the sociolegal context of parapolicing in Toronto. First, I explore in more detail the dichotomy of public versus private security, and the problems inherent to it, and reveal the tangled patchwork of surveillance that makes up the security industry. Second, I discuss in detail the laws relating to the work of the parapolice, including the Criminal Code and the Trespass to Property Act. Intelligarde security officers are trained to 'push the envelope' of the law when it comes to making arrests, using all the authority at their disposal. Third, I consider how Intelligarde has privatized (vertically integrated) the process of eviction by resorting to in-house paralegals. Fourth, I compare the mobilizations of the Metropolitan Toronto Police (MTP) with those of Intelligarde. Fifth and finally, I begin my ethnographic account of parapolicing by taking the reader on what Intelligarde security officers termed 'a trip through the sewer.'

Public vs Private Policing: The Problematic Dichotomy

Cooperation between the public and the private police is often facilitated by the migration of retiring police officers to the private security sector. This 'old boys' network' (Shearing, Farnell, and Stenning, 1980) is yet another mechanism for exchanging information between agencies. It should come as no surprise, for example, that Excalibur security – the firm contracted by the RCMP at Pearson International Airport – is owned and operated by a former RCMP officer. Relations between the public police and the private security sector have become so close that South East Florida police cadets receive security instruction as part of their standard training (Bottom and McCreedy, 1984). Police and security firms have sometimes formed cooperative associations to meet and discuss topics such as bomb threats, executive protection, and burglary investigation (Peterson, 1983).

The police are becoming not only institutional partners with private security firms – often under the umbrella of community-based policing – but also advocates for those firms. The International Association of Chiefs of Police (IACP) now has a liaison committee that devotes itself to strengthening ties with the private security sector, with the goal of '[giving] the police agency additional eyes and ears with which to locate wanted persons' (Hertig, 1986). Together, the IACP, and the American Society for Industrial Security (ASIS) draft model legislation and lobby for its passage. This legislation is geared towards allowing private firms access to police records as a tool in employee screening (Moulton, 1987). In Amarillo, Texas, the police and Allstate Security have worked out some interesting arrangements. In August 1981, Allstate assumed responsibility for responding to alarm calls everywhere in the city. Around the same time, the Amarillo police hired security officers to patrol the downtown core during peak hours, in tandem with the police. Today, 'most clients ... call Allstate on minor emergencies or prowler calls' (Pancake, 1983: 36). Similar programs have been established in New York City, where a police–private security liaison program now links police precincts with thirty security organizations in a 'structured anti-crime effort' (Bocklet, 1990). In Tacoma and Philadelphia (see Greene, Seamon, and Levy, 1995), as in Amarillo, private security guards are helping the police patrol downtown areas. Even more cogent examples can be found in Los Angeles; there, middle-class citizens/consumers have pooled their resources to build private residential enclaves, which are patrolled by armed private security guards (see Davis, 1990: Chapter 4). In Canada, closed developments like these has been mainly a regional phenomenon. British Columbia now has many gated communities.

The situation in shopping malls is just as interesting. Though they are 'public places' (albeit privately owned), most shopping malls are patrolled by private security personnel. However, under the rubric of community-based policing, more and more community police kiosks or storefronts are being installed within malls. The result is that police and private security agents are responsible for the same 'patches' (territories). In some situations the police alone are asked to patrol the mall on a contract basis, with the mall owners and the city sharing the costs (Rygier, 1983). In other situations the mall tenants bear all the costs. At North York's Jane-Finch mall, the MTP shares office space and even information and photographs about banned individuals with Intelligarde. Is it meaningful to call one police officer a private agent and the other a public agent on the basis of sponsorship? This is a long-standing question in the sociology of policing (Becker, 1974). There are clearly many difficulties associated with using sponsorship as grounds to differentiate between public and private policing. With shopping malls, Pearson International airport, and even downtown Toronto, this becomes glaringly obvious. Do a private security firm's purposes and operations vary significantly with the nature of the client? To a certain extent they do, but are these variations a function of whether the client is public or private? The answer again, I think, is not very clear. A private security firm does not cease being 'private' when hired by a state client. This is true even when the security firm is hired by the public police – a more and more commonplace arrangement. This is also true when pay-duty police officers are employed by private interests. In situations like this, the officer is being paid privately though a police association or union, and is earning extra income by selling his or her training, expertise, and most importantly, air of authority; but is still a state law enforcement officer. An officer who is sued for any malfeasance while under private contract is still insured by the municipality. In this way, taxpayers are subsidizing private policing. In essence, public police officers are being thrown onto the market as commodities in competition or cooperation with private security services. Yet another example of this is the RCMP contracting services in airports to the quasi-public Corps of Commissionaires and to private security firms.

In Sussex Borough, New Jersey the municipal police could no longer be afforded and were dissolved. The borough decided to rely on the state police, and hired a private security firm to provide a more constant uniformed presence. It became clear, however, that the security firm's actual mission was to act as an independent municipal police department. When the security officers immediately began issuing traffic tickets and summonses, and detaining and arresting suspects, the Sussex County prosecutor sought an injunction against the borough. In a published paper on the issue, this prosecutor noted that had the security firm constructed some hierarchy of accountability similar to that of the public police, and had its contract stipulated that competing firms should follow state guidelines for screening and training, the private contracting of policing would have been legal (O'Leary, 1994). Recently, the new Ontario municipality of Quinte West has entertained bids for policing from private security firms (Palango, 1998). Does this transform private security into public policing?

In Canada, 'strategic partnerships' (Normandeau and Leighton, 1990) with private security are becoming more and more common, under the rubric of community-based policing. Thirteen municipalities in the Montreal area hired security firms in response to a perceived lack of police patrol. Although the powers of these firms were limited mainly to enforcing parking bylaws, by 1987 at least nine municipalities had passed motions calling for private police officers to be granted powers to enforce moving traffic violations (Forcese, 1992: 113–14). Intelligarde International has contracts with Cityhome properties, the Toronto Economic and Development Corporation, the Toronto Parking Authority, and Peel Living. This means that Intelligarde polices a large share of the low-income housing in both Toronto and Mississauga, in addition to Toronto's harbour and beach areas and all of Toronto's ninety public parking lots. When one adds to all these the Cabbagetown properties alongside Metropolitan Toronto Housing Authority (MTHA)[2] buildings, the number of citizens under Intelligarde's purview is staggering.

In downtown Toronto, Intelligarde polices a neighbourhood the size of nine city blocks, bordered by Howard Street to the north, Wellesley Street to the south, Sherbourne Street to the west, and Parliament Street to the east. If we include the handful of MTHA buildings dotting the same territory, private agents are policing over 2 square kilometres of highrise buildings, walkways, and roadways, as well as over 30,000 working-class people in the heart of Toronto. The company has negotiated agreements with at least two different landowners of over a dozen building complexes that allow its security officers to leave sites unattended and assist their partners at adjacent properties as needed. This unique arrangement benefits all clients, since it means that culprits can be pursued, captured, and banned without fear of crime displacement.[3] It also creates a multicliented, multitasked, multiterritoried, cooperatively governed police service that closely mirrors the municipal police. Cityhome, Intelligarde's major downtown client is a publicly funded corporation with elected tenants' associations that oversee security provision. Intelligarde is functionally answerable to these associations:

Look, we're paid by Cityhome management but we're also paid by the tenants because they pay rent. Often, there are some subsidies involved, so in effect, the taxpayer also chips in for our services. Then, we're answerable to an elected and very political body called a tenant's association. One phone call from a disgruntled tenant association president to the property owner and we're in serious trouble. A couple more phone calls and we could lose a major contract. So it's our job to make sure these people are satisfied with their service ... Thàt means making arrests, cleaning up the streets, letting them know we care about their neighbourhood. The only difference between us and the cops is that we can get fired. But the way I figure it, if we're there, they've already been fired. (Intelligarde manager)

Add this to Intelligarde's law enforcement focus, and there are strong grounds to question the sense of distinguishing public from private police – this division becomes less and less meaningful.[4]

Just as convoluted is the question of legal status. Security guards and police officers in Canada are governed by separate legislation. In Ontario, security guards are governed by the Private Investigators and Security Guard Act (R.S.O. 1990), and the police by the Police Services Act (R.S.O. amended 1997). But besides police officers, security guards, and private investigators, there exist a litany of other law enforcement statuses: municipal law enforcement officers, Commissionaires, special constables, provincial offences officers, and a wide assortment of federal and provincial agents empowered by regulatory acts governing parklands, transportation, immigration, customs, and so on. All of these titles have typically been assigned to state bureaucracies or institutions with specific regulatory mandates. For example, university security services and parliamentary protective bodies are typically staffed by special constables.[5] There is nothing to suggest, however, that these statuses cannot alternate between public and private policing services, or that deployment governs legal status. On the contrary, many private security services in Ontario used to qualify their security officers as special constables so that they could issue parking tickets on private property. Along with the security officers' power to enforce municipal codes, however, came general 'peace officer' powers, usually reserved for public police services (Freedman and Stenning, 1977: 271–4; reprinted in Stenning and Shearing, 1979: Appendix A). Today a new status exists – the municipal law enforcement officer (MLEO) – for which authority is confined to municipal parking regulations. So it is not wise to link deployment or tasks to legal status. It is likely that large private security firms, and even in-house security bodies, make more arrests and engage in more order maintenance in downtown Toronto malls[6] and public places[7] than many police forces in sleepy suburban or rural Ontario. They do so routinely, without peace officer powers. The University of Toronto and York University have similar security requirements. At the U of T they are met by a police service (or special constabulary); at York, much to the officers' chagrin, there is a simple in-house security arrangement: 'The actual tasks performed by the coppers and the highly positive attitudes that they display toward their peace keeping and crime fighting work reinforce the strategy of achieving collective upward mobility by means of professionalization. Both their work and their occupational ideology buttress the pursuit of special constable status' (Micucci, 1994: 391; see also Miccuci, 1995). At Saint Mary's University in Halifax, Nova Scotia, where I teach, the quasi-public Corps of Commissionaires holds the security contract.

So while job tasks may in theory imply varying levels of policing status, this is not necessarily borne out in practice. On the contrary, local and extra-local security concerns are tempered by the judgments of individuals in positions of authority, who must make decisions about the needs of a given organization.

There are often greater differences between Intelligarde and other security firms than there are between Intelligarde and the MTP. While Intelligarde considers itself 'The Law Enforcement Company,'[8] executives from other security companies have serious reservations about this claim:

No. There's no overlap. We're a security company that provides a guard service and quite a lot of alarm response but I keep hearing you say policing – *private* policing – and we don't do that ... See, there are companies who take that on, who think they're police, but they're not. We don't go around harassing people. We are the eyes and ears of the police and management, and we safeguard properties, but we don't make arrests. That's not our job. (security executive)

Another executive, in the context of drawing a sharp distinction between his own firm and Intelligarde, showed outright disdain for his competitor and made an assortment of groundless accusations:

Yeah, Intelligarde, which is basically run by an ex-policeman who has close associations with certain divisions in the police force, who is trying to take on and lobby for taking on certain functions which are currently being provided by the police. Who [*sic*] is breaking laws right now, both in terms of their uniforming standard and their behaviour – literally. (security executive)

I do not intend to analyse outsiders' perceptions of Intelligarde until later chapters, but these comments illustrate clearly that Intelligarde is more different from other security companies than it is from the public police, in terms of both mobilization and mission. This is an important point, because earlier theorists have argued that private and public policing organizations have been governed by two very different logics: the police are concerned with crime control and *apprehension*, whereas private security agents are concerned with loss *prevention* (Shearing, Farnell, and Stenning, 1980; Stenning and Shearing, 1979: 16). It is assumed that the public police task themselves with 'good pinches,' whereas private security agents drop 'snowflakes'[9] in a more subtle form of coercion (Shearing and Stenning, 1982b). This is no longer the case, if it ever was. We know that in the history of the 'monied' police, these two duties were intertwined within a 'political economy of thief-taking' (McMullan, 1995):

> State rewards, unsystematic at first, eventually enhanced the role of monied police. Proclamations and orders from King and Parliament offered sums of money or commodities in kind to enterprising searchers. Neighbours and fellow tradesmen were encouraged to spy and turn evidence on each other ... In London, informing and thief-taking developed into specialized trades and came to prominence with the development of government rewards, inducements and pardons for checking crime and social unrest. (Emsley, 1987: 175; McMullan, 1995: 123, 125)

In today's neoconservative climate, private prisons, private prisoner transportation, private court security, private forensic accounting, private second-tier policing, and private security in expansive outdoor residential areas, have all been legitimated, and private policing is no longer just about loss prevention (Bayley and Shearing, 1996; Kempa et al., 1999). This is especially true when we consider the tremendous fear (Hollway and Jefferson, 1997) – especially of violent crime – that is endemic in neoliberal risk markets, and the tremendous aversion to risk. Traditional private security arrangements are as much about crime control as loss prevention; public policing is just as much about loss prevention as about apprehension. This latter dynamic is typified by public police cooperation with insurance companies, with the goal of minimizing loss (O'Malley, 1991), and by the new 'communications policing' (Ericson, Haggerty, and Carriere, 1993). Both approaches are geared toward encouraging the public to police themselves. Ironically a process of 'responsibilization' – well entrenched among private corporate logics – is seeking to relieve corporate élites and police managers of their ethical and litigious liability. This downloading of responsibility fuels unease among the general workforce, and in neighbourhoods and other purchasing collectives; this in turn elicits further demands for protection against industrial accidents, crime, and intrusion which in turn accelerates the need for commodified security.

The pursuit of security, then, is both a state business and a corporate one. The National Institute of Justice's report on 'measuring what matters' in policing (Greene, 1997) reflects a strengthening trend toward the corporatization of state institutions (including welfare). The jingoism of the free market has infiltrated the logics of public police management as the need to justify resources becomes paramount. How does a police chief justify cost, improve products, diversify his or her product line, and compete with the industry norm? How different are these operational decisions from the determinations being made by private security managers across the globe? Consider here especially that public and private police agencies no longer secure different populations, territories, or markets. 'We're looking at where this industry is going and where individual firms in the marketplace are,' notes Greene (1997: 8). Police chiefs are no longer traditional managers – even their titles are being reimagined, with some now being referred to as chief executive officers (see also Loader, 1999).

It is also more difficult than one might think to label police services as either 'public' and 'private' on the basis of the profit motive. Canada's federal police force, the RCMP, actively seeks out contracts – an entrenched historical practice – in an increasingly lucrative and competitive market. The Solicitor General sends out circulars promoting the RCMP product that sounds eerily like the marketing materials used by private firms:

> With more than a century of expertise, co-operation and respect to build on, and a national infrastructure that extends from the nation's smallest, remotest communities to the international level, the RCMP is equipped to deliver objective, efficient and sympathetic policing services ... The RCMP provides excellent provincial and municipal policing at a cost equal to or less than what its contract partners would have to spend on police forces of their own. (Solicitor General Canada, 1996)

With success that most corporate executives would envy, the Solicitor

General has gradually retreated from funding contracted police services. Between 1928 and 1966 the federal government paid for 60 per cent of local or provincial policing budgets. By 1990 the federal share was only 30 per cent, and it continues to decrease by 1 or 2 per cent a year (Solicitor General Canada, 1996). With an annual budget of $1 billion and a staff of 10,400 officers and civilians delivering services under contract, the RCMP brings the government $700 million in revenue every year (Solicitor General Canada, 1996). Though it still suffers a net loss of $300 million a year, through a process of 'vote netting' it recovers this loss from general government revenues. The long-term goal of RCMP contract policing is 100 per cent cost recovery.

Today the RCMP competes for contracts directly, because the federal government no longer subsidizes the contract services they provide. All 'expansions' in contract services must be 'cost neutral' to the federal government. Thus, when the RCMP 'won' the municipal policing contract for Moncton, New Brunswick, it did so by bidding with 100 per cent of the proposed cost to them (personal communication: Staff Sgt Barry Dunn, Policing Contract Services, Finance Branch, 3 July 1998). And in many jurisdictions in British Columbia, the local 'partners' (read: clients) pay between 90 and 100 per cent of the policing costs. In sum, public police services are now actively competing with private firms in both mature and newly emerging risk markets. Intelligarde International is hoping that local police services will subcontract Tier II policing to them, for the sake of cost efficiency.

It should now be clear that many factors make it hard for us to draw accurate distinctions between public and private policing. Johnston (1992: 195–6) has suggested that it is most sensible to locate policing institutions along two axes: public to private, and local to supranational (see his Figure 9.1). As I noted earlier, however, this does not tell us all there is to know about different forms of policing. Just as important as sponsorship may be functional accountability, the environment being policed, the frequency of detentions and/or arrests, legal status, training, whether they are armed, and even uniforming. These are equally important factors in gaining compliance from the public. There have even been discussions about whether the mandate of Toronto's Police Services Board should be abolished, with responsibility for policing functions shifted to city council, and by incorporating private security companies the better to oversee them (Stenning, 1997). This has already happened in some jurisdictions. In Nova Scotia, the Police Commission sets aside time in its itinerary to hear complaints against private security guards licensed in the province. In practical terms, public and private security are now so tightly linked that even police research centres have been proposed with this overlapping function in mind, as in the case of York University's Centre for Police and Security Studies (Eustace, 1992).

More and more, the new parapolice are rendering the public-private distinction meaningless from an analytic perspective. They say they are not concerned merely with loss prevention. They contend that they are actively engaging the new risk markets of urban fear and shrinking state budgets to redefine policing. They are taking advantage of neoliberal rationales and selling themselves not only as viable additions to the public police but also as alternatives. Organizations like these are typified in North America by 'law enforcement companies' such as Intelligarde International. In the remainder of this book I will spend a lot of time testing these pronouncements and their implications. To a certain extent, the adjective 'new' preceding the noun 'parapolice' is a misnomer. This is because there is a historical precedent for parapolicing arrangements, especially in British policing. Notwithstanding this, I want to draw specific attention to new developments in societal demands for changing security forms and in the industry's responses to those demands.[10]

Powers of the Parapolice

We don't have special powers. Everybody always asks us where we get our authority from. I've been to contract bids, presentations, with even a cop on the panel – a police officer and he should know better – and he asked the same stupid question: 'You guys aren't cops, how can you do all the things you promise?' Well, we just do our job and we use the powers every citizen and every landowner already has. It isn't magic, it just takes guts. It takes training. It takes skill. And it takes a company that will back up their officers if someone wants to sue. We are that company. It's what we like to call 'pushing the envelope.' (Intelligarde manager)

I do not intend, in this section, to present an exhaustive summary of case law concerning the limits of search, seizure, arrest, and detention powers for security personnel. This has been expertly considered elsewhere (Stenning and Shearing, 1979; Rigakos and Greener, 2000). Instead, I want to discuss briefly the sociolegal context in which Intelligarde security officers ply their trade. In later chapters I will examine more closely how the enabling and disabling qualities of these powers affect Intelligarde security officers' job satisfaction, and lead to malaise within a 'wannabe' culture. What I want to do now is offer a basic understanding of the legal devices that Intelligarde security staff employ on a daily basis. It will quickly become obvious that Intelligarde staff do not have special powers. What they do have is an organizational philosophy, and a willingness to 'push the envelope' with the powers they do have.

To understand security work in Ontario, one must first understand the concept of private property ownership. Every person in a capitalist society has the incontrovertible 'right' to own property, and the related right to the exclusive enjoyment of that property without trespass. In Ontario this entitlement is ensured by the Trespass to Property Act (R.S.O. 1980, c.511). Under s.9(1) of this Act 'a police officer, or the occupier of the premises, *or a person authorized by the occupier* may arrest without warrant any person he believes on reasonable and probable grounds to be on the premises in contravention of section 2.' Section 2 of the Trespass to Property Act makes explicit the grounds for an arrest:

> 2(1) Every person who is not acting under a right of authority conferred by law and who,
>> (a) without the express permission of the occupier, the proof which rests on the defendant,
>>> (i) enters on premises when entry is prohibited under this Act, or
>>> (ii) engages in an activity on premises when the activity is prohibited under this Act; or
>> (b) does not leave the premises immediately after he is directed to do so by the occupier of the premises or a person authorized by the occupier
>
> is guilty of an offence and on conviction is liable to a fine of not more than $1,000.

In other words, when an individual enters an area of private property to which access is restricted by either notice or sign or physical barrier (s.3), that person may be arrested for trespassing. It follows that a security officer who is an agent of the landowner is entitled to arrest any individual who enters a private space expressly prohibited under s.2(a)(i) of the Act. Intelligarde officers are schooled to 'read them their rights.' A security guard, like any private citizen or peace officer, must inform suspects that they are under arrest, what they are under arrest for, that they may remain silent, and that they have a right to retain counsel (see s.10 of the Constitution Act).

A more interesting situation arises when a person is on a property *with* permission (i.e., access is open to the public) but is engaging in 'prohibited' activity. Obviously, there are different interpretations of *prohibited*. The word certainly covers all criminal offences, and may also include municipal bylaws and provincial regulations. But what about actions that simply offend the sensibilities of the landowner? As far as Intelligarde officers are concerned, prohibited activity includes anything they can justify as 'immoral, illegal, or unethical.' Section 2(1)(b) of the Act grants security agents tremendous discretion by allowing them to ask a person to leave a property without having to provide a reason. In practice, however, this section of the Act is typically used to avoid having to make an arrest. For instance, when someone is being loud or boisterous on private property and this is not permitted, that person can be arrested immediately under s.2(1)(a)(ii) for engaging in prohibited activity, or can be asked to leave. If the 'troublemaker' refuses, the security officer can arrest under s.2(1)(a)(ii) or s.2(1)(a)(b) of the Act. Intelligarde officers are instructed that they should ask a person leave the property at least three times before making an arrest under s.2(1)(a)(b); otherwise, the courts might view their actions as overzealous. These sweeping powers are often buttressed by various other enabling mechanisms. Strategically placed signs prohibiting certain activities on private property can further extend a private security guard's grounds for arrest. While there is nothing at any level of public governance that makes loitering explicitly illegal, a well-placed sign makes it a prohibited activity on private property and allows a security guard to either immediately arrest undesirable people or ask them to leave. If the offenders resist, they can then be arrested under s.2(1)(a)(b) of the Act. In other words, courts might frown on private lawmaking through the arbitrary posting of signs, but they cannot very well take away a landowner's right to remove individuals from property found in direct violation of a prohibited activity. If those individuals refuse to leave, the landowner has the right to arrest them, and so does the landowner's agent.

No matter what the grounds for arrest – and they seem nearly limitless – the private landowner or that landowner's agents must turn over an arrested individual to the police:

> 9(2) Where a person who makes an arrest under subsection (1) is not a police officer, he shall promptly call for assistance a police officer and give the person into custody of the police officer.

Of course, the police do not always proceed with charges against the individual and this sometimes leads to tension and frustration among Intelligarde security staff. When a police officer takes the arrest seriously, the security officer receives a sense of validation. Often, less serious (i.e., noncriminal) offences are handled by issuing notices prohibiting entry (NPEs), so as not to involve the police in trivial matters. This allows the security guard additional discretion; the police are called only for more serious offences.

Thus, instead of arresting someone immediately, the security agent may issue 'sufficient notice' to that person 'orally or in writing' under s.5(1) of the Act. Almost invariably, banishments are handled using NPEs: in the twelve months between August 1996 and September 1997, Intelligarde staff issued 2,617 NPEs. NPEs begin an important paper trail that makes it easier, or more justifiable, to arrest someone after a second or third trespass incident. An individual who returns to a site from which he or she has been banned by an NPE no matter what the reason (save for exercising some legally sanctioned act), can be arrested under s.2(1)(a)(ii).[11] Intelligarde staff photograph banned individuals at each site; they also file all NPEs at headquarters; these individuals are entered into an electronic database for future reference. If an Intelligarde officer obtains the name of a suspicious person he believes has been banned from a property, he may radio dispatch for confirmation and decide whether to issue an NPE or arrest the trespasser.

A second arrest power for security personnel stems from general Criminal Code provisions that entitle citizens to make arrests. In many ways this power is redundant for private security agents, since they can already arrest for prohibited activity on the private properties they police. This power is extended, however, to all properties, whether public or private, when a criminal offence is occurring:

> 494. (1) Any one may arrest without warrant
>   (a) a person whom he finds committing an indictable offence; or
>   (b) a person who, on reasonable an probable grounds, he believes
>   (i) has committed a criminal offence, and
>   (ii) is escaping from and freshly pursued by persons who have lawful authority to arrest that person.

Landowners are specifically mentioned in the Criminal Code, but there is nothing that extends the powers of arrest for private security agents beyond those already provided for in Ontario's Trespass to Property Act:

494. (2) Any one who is
   (a) the owner or a person in lawful possession of property, or
   (b) a person authorized by the owner or by a person in lawful pos-
       session of property
may arrest without warrant a person whom he finds committing a criminal
offence on or in relation to that property.

As with the Trespass Act, anyone arrested by a citizen must be turned
over to a peace officer (s.494(3)). The main difference between private
citizens' powers of arrest and those afforded police officers is that the
latter may arrest on suspicion that an indictable offence has been or will
be committed. The Criminal Code has various other sections containing
redundant powers of arrest. These relate to defence of dwelling (s.40),
defence of movable property (s.38) and defence of house or real property (s.41). A property owner or that owner's agent can arrest for assault
if a trespasser refuses to return property or to leave the premises. These
sections of the Criminal Code are rarely if ever used by Intelligarde
security officers.

Search and seizure powers are limited mainly to peace officers in Canada, although common law judgments have allowed searches by private
persons for weapons or evidence immediately after the arrest of suspects
(Stenning and Shearing, 1979: 62–3).[12] Intelligarde security officers
know that searches for weapons are admissible but that consent should
be obtained to avoid legal difficulties. Typically, this consent is forthcoming. As in other jurisdictions (Sarre, 1994), a security officer's uniform
and appearance of authority can do much to elicit compliance from the
public. Intelligarde officers are instructed to leave all evidence, other
than weapons, in the suspects' pockets. When the police arrive, they discreetly indicate to the responding officer that narcotics were found in a
particular pocket or item of clothing. This alleviates the legal uncertainty
of searches by private persons. It also

makes [Intelligarde look like] very cooperative campers in the eyes of the
police. We make their jobs easier. I'm sure the paperwork and case processing
would be much more difficult if a security guard walked up to them with some
crack in his hand and said, 'Look what I found.' This way we don't even have to
testify – it's entirely a police matter, and we're more than happy to give them all
the credit. (static security officer – male)

In short, the most well-worn piece of legislation for Intelligarde staff is the

Trespass to Property Act. It provides them with broad powers of arrest on private property and is the statute of choice among a litany of provisions making it very easy for private security guards to arrest citizens in Ontario. (Various federal provisions may be used from time to time.) The Trespass to Property Act gives Intelligarde officers wide-ranging grounds to arrest someone before handing them over to the public police. After the police arrive, an entirely new set of enabling recipe rules (Ericson, 1982; McBarnet, 1981) can be deployed to process the suspect.

Private Justice

Intelligarde offers legal services to its clients in actions against tenants or trespassers. Pursuing an eviction case through the courts is a long and complicated process of serving summonses and notices. Often, clients are intimidated or are too busy to deal with tenants, and so hire paralegals to conduct the litigation. Unfortunately, paralegals too are often afraid to enter high-crime areas or to knock on the doors of possible or known drug dealers. At one time, Intelligarde contracted out its paralegal matters, but it found that the cases were not handled with due diligence. So instead, management sponsored a company employee for paralegal training. For the last three years most of Intelligarde's routine legal proceedings have been handled by an in-house paralegal.

The actual title of Intelligarde's legal worker is 'commissioner.' This allows him to swear affidavits and conduct oaths. The company also employs a deputy commissioner with similar responsibilities.[13] Intelligarde's commissioner can appear for pretrial motions, set dates, and interview witnesses. This capability helps offset any legal fees; it also ensures that the company is represented during proceedings that are perceived to be vindictive and/or unsubstantiated:

There have been six cases against us on private countercharges, and we usually present medical records showing our guys were attacked. Many days they'll wait for the last day of the sixth month to lay a private information. Twice they waited until the last day ... During the OCAP scandal, I appeared for the guys involved. They have already brought a total of five charges against us, but the police hate them even more than they hate us. (Intelligarde paralegal)

Given how difficult and time-consuming it is to proceed with an eviction, it is little wonder that the Law Enforcement Company has elected to employ in-house counsel for its clients. The first step in the process involves issuing a notice of termination, in which a reason for the eviction must be stipulated. Reasons can include rent in arrears, breach of obligation, illegal parties in the apartment, illegal activities on the property, general breaches of the Landlord and Tenant Act, or contractual violations. If a tenant has committed a criminal act – as is so often the case in Intelligarde-sponsored proceedings – he or she must be given twenty days to vacate the premises. Typically, however, the tenant receives an additional forty days from the courts.

When the tenant does not leave, a Notice of Application and an Affidavit of Service are filed with the landlord-tenant court specifying why the tenant should be removed. A pretrial date is set three weeks to a month after the notice is submitted. If the tenant does not appear for the pretrial hearing, a default judgment is entered; if the tenant appears, the case must be referred to a judge, since the registrar does not have judicial authority. This first default judgment can later be turned aside because it has not been issued by a judge. A trial date is then set a few weeks from the date of the appearance before the registrar. If the tenant appears for the trial, the judicial process is underway. If the tenant does not appear, another default judgment is filed that cannot be turned aside. The judgment is received two weeks later by the landlord (or the landlord's agent). The tenant is then served. Eight days later, the landlord must go to the original court and file a Right of Possession, a Requisition to the Sheriff, an information sheet pertaining to the unit (needed by the police), and an Affidavit of Service indicating when the judgment was served with the court clerk. Three weeks later an information sheet is presented to the landlord. Then finally, the sheriff can take action. Even at this stage, the papers may be questioned if they contain a registrar's affidavit and not a judge's. An *ex parte* hearing may be called so that evidence and updated information can be filed in support of the affidavit.

These eviction proceedings can take as long as six months. In the environment of parapolicing, the municipal police and paralegals are bypassed as a service to the consumer. In effect, Intelligarde is supplying a vertically integrated and operationally autonomous justice system for its clients – a commodified system of policing that seeks to satiate a risk market.

Public vs Private Law Enforcement: A Statistical Comparison

So far I have presented an inventory of arguments and examples, both conceptual and practical, that support the contention that there is sym-

Intelligarde security officers 'swarm' a building during a TIP.

Deister checkpoints exemplify the late capitalist compulsion to translate immaterial (and 'unproductive') security labour into a tangible commodity.

Self-defence training demonstration. Intelligarde officers are trained by a law enforcement expert.

Intelligarde manager scrutinizes Deister patrol reports. The system attempts to order the chaos of satellite sites and workers. Security officers 'ghost' within the system in order to circumvent it.

'Suspicious persons' are stopped and questioned at Intelligarde buildings. Thirty-five per cent of persons banned have no fixed address.

Over 45 per cent of males and only 9 per cent of females receive handgun training at Intelligarde.

Shift activity reports are overviewed in order for platoons to produce more Deister 'hits.'

An ethic of mutual assistance is central to the wannabe subculture.

Communication centre staff monitor the activities of both mobile and static officers. Informal arrangements often subvert this surveillance practice.

Armed and canine protection during money drop-offs at a Toronto mall.

Training for public order policing on private property.

metry between public and private *para*policing functions and operations. It does no good, however, to simply employ the rhetorics of
parapolicing – be they corporate, communitarian,[14] or even militaristic
– as unassailable evidence that private and public law enforcement are
congruent. I have argued throughout this book that such approaches
have limitations. In this section I offer a statistical comparison of the
mobilizations of Intelligarde International and the Metropolitan Toronto Police Service, as only an initial indication of the 'reality' of similarities between the two policing organizations. In later sections and
chapters, I will offer ethnographic data to expand on these opening
observations.

The data I present in Table 3.1 are derived from many sources and
should be read cautiously. The table compares largely non-comparable
measures, reflecting variations in institutional contexts, methods of collection, and periods of coverage. The MTP figures are taken from that
organization's 1995 Annual Report (Metropolitan Toronto Police Service, 1995a).[15] The data for Intelligarde are based on occurrence report
files, alarm response frequencies, banning data, personnel files, and
interviews with management. It can hardly be ignored that the public
police and the parapolice do not engage in identical mobilizations. For
one thing, the parapolice cannot issue tickets for moving traffic violations or provincial offences. For another, they do not do homicide investigations or other major crime work. But, of course, *most* police officers
also don't engage in these two functions: most traffic and criminal investigations work has been hived off into specialized units. However, the
overall data should not 'isolate away' these operational differences.
Because an Intelligarde officer is exponentially more likely to make a
'drug' arrest than a member of a rural Ontario police service, does this
mean that comparisons are unfair? Of course not – the data simply
reflect an anticipated outcome based on, in this case, the environment
being policed. The data are artefacts of different police mobilizations.
This begs us to ask whether the parapolice engage in as much crime
control as many public police (or in this case more). In short, the data
in their aggregate form are a more or less sound approximation of the
daily routines of both policing services.

The data presented in Table 3.1 relate to three important elements of
policing: (1) 'busy-ness,' or the rate of mobilization; (2) the chances of
being disciplined, fired, or having legal processes initiated against public or parapolice officers; and (3) the likelihood of being injured in the
line of duty. These categories represent what many police sociologists

have identified as the three central indredients of the police occupational culture. Manning (1997) views danger and sacrifice as central
components in the 'drama' of doing police work. The police in isolation
– as unsung heroes – are typified in Manning's treatment of the police
funeral. Other researchers have looked directly at the 'reproducing'
nature of police mobilizations (Ericson, 1982), or at the tremendous
impact of paperwork (Ericson and Haggerty, 1997), or have specifically
identified important components of the police subculture: danger,
authority, and the need to look busy (Skolnick, 1966). The available
sources of information permit comparisons across the following opera-
tionalized items: (1) OMPR: the organizational mobilization and processing ratio, (2) PAUR: the proceedings against uniform officers ratio,
and (3) DIRU: the dangerous incident rate per uniform officer.

Each of the three items of comparison needs careful explanation.
The OMPR is the amount of official paperwork filed about or against
citizens being policed, divided by the number of uniformed officers in
the organization. Basically, the OMPR reflects how busy (officially) the
average officer is in a calendar year. Of course, I had to calculate this
ratio differently for the two organizations because of differences in their
reporting procedures. At the same time, I had to maintain the epistemic
relationship between nominal ('being busy') and operational defini-
tions (OMPR) (Palys, 1992: 403). I calculate the OMPR for the Toronto
Police by totalling all Criminal Code charges ($n = 54,715$), drug charges
($n = 6,438$) (Food and Drug Act, Narcotic Control Act), other federal
statute charges ($n = 1,162$), Liquor Licence Act charges ($n = 2,477$),
other provincial charges ($n = 9,823$), and municipal bylaw charges ($n =
2,429$) in 1995. I then divided this sum ($\Sigma = 77,044$) by the number of
uniformed police officers ($n = 5,059$). The OMPR for Intelligarde was a
little more difficult to calculate. I added the number of occurrence
reports filed ($n = 1,703$) to the number of total bannings ($n = 2,617$),
first, however, reducing the occurrence total by 30.6 per cent: 13.5 per
cent for the number of NPEs issued and a further 17.1 per cent for the
number of outcomes indicating arrest and banning. This eliminated
overlap with the bannings database and reduced the number of occurrences to 1,180. I then divided this new sum ($\Sigma = 3,797$) of bannings and
occurrences by the number of Intelligarde uniformed staff ($n = 141$).

The PAUR indicates the average uniformed officer's chances of having
proceedings launched against him or her. It is an attempt to measure the
actual risk of internal reprimand – in other words, to quantify the often
noted 'siege mentality' in the police subculture. It also helps us measure

the use of force by the public police, and the public's hostility against them. I calculate the PAUR for the MTP by totalling the cases where formal proceedings were launched against uniformed officers through either the chief's discretion – which includes criminal charges ($n = 3$), disciplinary charges ($n = 3$), and third-party counsel or caution ($n = 6$) – or proceedings launched by Complaints Bureau dispositions resulting in some resolution other than withdrawal ($n = 106$). In then divided this sum ($\Sigma = 115$) by the number of uniformed officers ($n = 5,059$) and multiplied by 100. This final figure reflected each police officer's percentage chance of ever suffering reprimand, caution, or criminal charges. Such structured forms of accountability are not in place for security guards in Ontario. There are, however, a number of other specialized and non-specialized forms of accountability. The OPP Registrar is an obvious body of oversight, but its actions are typically against firms rather than individual security officers. On the other hand, security companies do not have immunity from litigation, whether criminal and civil. This often results in civil suits against firms or the laying of 'private informations' against individual security guards. From the perspective of Intelligarde's parapolice, this is a frequent occurrence. So to measure PAUR for Intelligarde, I added the number of criminal legal challenges[16] against the firm in the last fifteen years ($n = 55$) divided by 15 to arrive at a yearly average indicator of official sanctions beginning in the public courts. I then added this number to the number of internally initiated dismissals in the previous year ($n = 6$),[17] then rounded off, and then divided by the number of uniformed staff ($n = 141$) and multiplied by 100.

In the 'police myth' (Manning, 1997: 45) of immanent danger, risk and policing are believed to go hand in hand. The DIRU seeks to quantify an officer's likelihood of being assaulted, attacked and/or injured on the job. A direct comparison of Worker's Injury and Safety Board (WISB) claims for the MTP and Intelligarde would have yielded the most accurate and reliable information about job-related injuries. Regrettably, the MTP refused my request for access to this information, even in the form of aggregate statistics. For the MTP I calculated the DIRU by dividing the number of offences against police officers ($n = 1,083$) by the number of dispatched calls ($n = 715,768$) and multiplying by 100. Ascertaining the DIRU for Intelligarde required some creativity, since the number of injuries to officers is not systematically recorded. I gleaned the percentage of injuries to security officers from a systematic random sample of occurrence reports (2.4 per cent), and then multiplied by the total number of those reports ($n = 1,703$). I then added the

TABLE 3.1
Public versus private police organizational mobilization characteristics

Comparative calculation	MTP†	Intelligarde‡
Organizational mobilization and processing ratio (OMPR)	15.23	26.93
Proceedings against uniformed officers ratio (PAUR)	2.27	6.86
Dangerous incident rate per uniformed officer (DIRU)	.151	.748

†Based on Metropolitan Toronto Police Service Annual Report (1995) statistics.
‡Based on occurrence report files, alarm response frequencies, banning database, and personnel files.

resulting figure to the number of assaults against security officers noted in the bannings database ($n = 12$), and divided by the total number of dispatched calls ($n = 2,628$ alarms[18] + 1,703 occurrences + 2,617 bannings = 6,948). I then divided the sum of assaults against officers ($\Sigma = 52$) by the total number of dispatched calls, and multiplied by 100. The number derived from all these calculations estimates the percentage chance that an officer will be attacked or assaulted when responding to a call, whether dispatched from headquarters or addressing an occurrence that arises while on patrol.

The final calculations presented in Table 3.1 yield some surprising conclusions. First, the OMPR score for Intelligarde is much higher than that of the MTP. This suggests that Intelligarde officers are more active in processing individuals and filing information about those contacts. There are a number of caveats, however, that should be added to this finding. Police officers may spend more time actually *filing* paperwork. Ericson and Haggerty (1997) report that officers spend large amounts of shiftwork completing mountains of redundant paperwork on behalf of a number of outside agencies. This may help explain why many less serious charges are not processed – the police choose to handle them informally. Also the relatively simple reporting formats of the parapolice may not require such a heavy investment of time. Nonetheless, the *opportunity* to be busy must be exponentially higher for the public police since the calculations presented in Table 3.1 also include traffic violations and the enforcement of various provincial statutes not within the realm of the parapolice. Parking ticket issuances are not included for either police body. To extend the argument even further, some percentage of official MTP charges must reflect cases brought to their attention by arrests made by Intelligarde. All these factors notwithstanding, the high OMPR figure for Intelligarde demonstrates that organization's impressive social control function.

Interestingly, the public police and Intelligarde officers are equally likely to have to defend themselves from formal legal proceedings launched by outsiders. But when one folds in informal and internal dismissals carried out by Intelligarde management, the parapolice are three times more likely to suffer from proceedings being launched against them. This lends credence to the notion that as parapolicing organizations take on more and more responsibility for raiding crack houses, arresting drug sellers and users, and clearing neighbourhoods, they will encounter the same civic resistance as the public police. Ironically, criticisms of 'Gestapo tactics,' racism, and beating down the poor have actually helped legitimize Intelligarde as a bona fide police agency, with all the troubles and resistance that role entails.

Without a doubt, the most striking finding in comparing Intelligarde to the public police is the vast difference in the DIRU: Intelligarde officers are five times more likely to be attacked in the course of their duties than MTP officers. This is vitally important when it comes to comparing the 'airs of authority' these two organisations carry. Because of their lack of legal standing, private security officers may have difficulty dealing with non-compliant detainees and angry observers. Perhaps most importantly, this last finding meshes perfectly with the perceptions of Intelligarde officers, who are in constant fear of being outnumbered in a surprise assault:

Afraid? Well, I guess if I had to say, I'd say the worst thing I worry about is being outnumbered. Have you talked to [H]? He'll tell you man, these fuckers can jump out of nowhere. I know that I can handle one guy or maybe two. If I'm in charge I can talk them down ... but sometimes, I guess, yeah, the worst thing is being swarmed. (static security officer – male)

I fear lack of back-up. That the guys won't get there in time and I'll be dead. You know, I often wonder what would happen if one of us died, you know. The cops get this big funeral procession and stuff. I wonder what [R] would give us? [*Laughter*] But I mean, it's not an unjustified fear – I wouldn't call it fear, it's more like caution – that you might get jumped. It depends on the security officer. I have good relations with everybody ... but then you never know. (mobile security officer – male)

Oh that's easy. Up in this area we've had problems. Not too long ago a guy got swarmed and some of them had weapons ... so that's what everyone around here is worried about. There are five guys here today, but what about next month when you're up here alone? That's why you need a good dog. (static site officer – male)

It is little wonder that 'back-up' is so central to the occupational code for Intelligarde officers. This code requires the parapolice to bend the rules to get to a scene quickly when requested. It also contributes to what I will later analyse as the 'swarm or be swarmed' occupational ethic. Furthermore, the mettle of most rookies is tested by their willingness to handle situations without having to constantly call for assistance.

So we now have some statistical foundation (albeit limited) for arguing that the parapolice, in function and in mobilization, are quite similar to the public police. In fact, there are grounds to argue that parapolicing is just as relevant to crime prevention as public policing – that it has transcended past perceptions of the security sector as responsible solely for loss prevention. Indeed, the above analysis indicates that Intelligarde officers are just as likely as police officers to face legal proceedings, and are five times more likely to be assaulted while on duty.

If the parapolice are active private law enforcement officers (as they themselves are quick to assert), what exactly is it that they do? Do they often get involved in 'real' crime control activities? If so, how often do they make arrests absent public police interventions? An examination of Intelligarde's occurrence report files yields some interesting answers to these questions (see Table 3.2). First, the most common reasons for parapolice mobilization relate to tenant noise complaints or information (17.1 per cent), followed closely by violence and disputes (15.3 per cent) and theft-related occurrences (12.9 per cent). Intelligarde officers spent the largest part of their time stopping forced entries and enforcing vagrancy-related offences (these situations represent 22.4 per cent of occurrence reports). With this in mind, we must consider what incidents prompt Intelligarde officers to make arrests and/or call for police assistance, because this will identify important mobilization characteristics of the parapolice (see Table 3.3). While tenant complaints or information may be the most frequent occurrence, they rarely result in Intelligarde (0 per cent) or public police (6.9 per cent) arrests. In fact, most arrests on Intelligarde properties involve vagrancy (100 per cent). The public police are called in only 26.3 per cent of such cases. The most common reasons to call the police were prohibited or forced entries (78.9 per cent) – so that POTs (provincial offence tickets) might be issued – violence and disputes (73.1 per cent), theft (76.2 per cent), and drug-

TABLE 3.2
Types of occurrences on Intelligarde properties

Occurrence type		n	%
Tenant complaint or info.	I	58	17.1
Violence and disputes	II	52	15.3
Theft related	III	44	12.9
Prohibited or forced entry	IV	38	11.2
Vagrancy related	V	38	11.2
Assist public agency	VI	36	10.6
Suspicious or threatening behaviour	VII	30	8.8
Maintenance related	VIII	22	6.5
Vandalism/mischief	IX	14	4.1
Drug related	X	8	2.4

Based on systematic random sample (n = 340) of company occurrence report files (N = 1,703) (at 95% confidence interval, p = .05, precision = ±5%). Items re-categorized from 42 incident types listed in order of frequency: I = noise complaint, info. from tenant, found person, found property; II = domestic dispute, common assault, assault security officer, sexual assault, tenant dispute, assault with weapon, deaths; III = theft under, vehicle break-in, attempt theft, fraud, stolen vehicle; IV = previously banned – arrested; forced entry, attempt forced entry; V = loitering, soliciting/panhandling, drunkenness; VI = fire alarm, medical emergency, vehicle accident; VII = suspicious person, suspicious activity, obscene calls, threats; VIII = insecure door, safety hazard, health hazard, leaks, floods, elevator maint., door maint., fire hazard; IX = vandalism, misuse fire equip., vandalize fire equip.; X = suspicious drug activity, drug abuse.

related incidents (50.0 per cent). Caution must be exercised with these percentages, since they reflect only reported (or officially observed) occurrences rather than the actual number of incidents. It is highly unlikely, for example, that vagrancy would be observed, with no action taken, and an occurrence report subsequently filed. Not only is this not worthy of reporting, but it might also reveal a security officer's less than vigilant disposition.

Statistics gleaned from an analysis of Intelligarde occurrence reports indicate that 32.4 per cent of occurrences result in arrest, and that 17.1 per cent of suspects are handed over to the police after banning. An additional 8.2 per cent of incidents involve assisting the public police in making arrests (see Table 3.4). By additionally tallying all public agency responses to Intelligarde-secured properties, we find that the police, ambulance, and the fire departments account for 37.9 per cent, 8.2 per cent, 5.9 per cent of responses respectively (see Table 3.5). This clearly establishes that the public police and Intelligarde International rou-

TABLE 3.3
Incidents prompting arrests and/or police assistance

	Arrest or detain		Police called	
Occurrence type	N	%	N	%
Tenant complaint or info. (N = 58)	0	0	4	6.9
Violence and disputes (N = 52)	14	26.9	38	73.1
Theft related (N = 44)	12	27.3	32	76.2
Prohibited or forced entry (N = 38)	22	57.9	30	78.9
Vagrancy related (N = 38)	38	100	10	26.3
Assist public agency (N = 36)	2	5.6	2	5.6
Suspicious or threatening behaviour (N = 30)	16	53.3	8	26.7
Maintenance related (N = 22)	0	0	0	0
Vandalism/mischief (N = 14)	0	0	0	0
Drug related (N = 8)	6	75.0	4	50.0

Based on systematic random sample (n = 340) of company occurrence report files (N = 1,703) (at 95% confidence interval, p = .05, precision = ±5%).

tinely interact. In both philosophy and practice, Intelligarde acts like a police force. To illustrate this point, there is no better way than what one Intelligarde officer called a 'trip through the sewer.'

A 'Trip through the Sewer'

At around 1:30 a.m. on a Wednesday night, I am driven to an Intelligarde site near the corner of Dundas and Sherbourne streets in downtown Toronto. As we turn up the driveway leading to the front of the residential building, the mobile officer escorting me points to a dark, stocky figure emerging from the lobby and smiles, 'There he is.' After being greeted at the door, we complete the obligatory introductions and the two co-workers begin to trade company gossip. I have by now grown accustomed to these discussions – Who is up for what stage of which police recruiting process? What was the last major incident involving violence? Who has been assigned to what duty? – and decide not to take notes. I begin my patrol with P, the officer on duty at this site, and we make arrangements to meet up with C when he returns from another 'hit.'

P: So what are you doing exactly?
Me: I'm studying private policing.
P: For what?

TABLE 3.4
Reported results of occurrences on properties secured by Intelligarde

Occurrence result	n	%
Arrest or detain	110	32.4
No arrest	230	67.6
Security officer action(s)		
Investigate and report	96	28.2
Arrest, ban, and turn over to police	58	17.1
NPE issued	46	13.5
Warning/keep the peace	49	11.8
Assist police	28	8.2
Unsubstantiated	20	5.9
Assist Fire Dept.	14	4.1
Assist ambulance	12	3.5
Suspect escaped	10	2.9
Escort from property	8	2.4
Assist police in effecting an arrest	6	1.8
Verbal banning	2	.6
Weapons		
None	318	93.5
Stick, bat, or blunt object(s)	12	3.5
Gun	6	1.8
Knife	4	1.2
Injuries		
None	294	86.5
Victim or other	32	9.4
Security officer(s)	8	2.4
Suspect(s)	4	1.2

Based on systematic random sample ($n = 340$) of company occurrence report files ($N = 1,703$), (at 95% confidence interval, $p = .05$, precision = ±5%). NPE = notice prohibiting entry.

Me: It's for my degree. I'm studying what you guys do and how every-
thing operates. You know, how you do your jobs and such.
P: And so ... what do you think?
Me: Well, I don't know yet, otherwise I wouldn't need to be here, right?
P: OK, well, let me show you around a bit.

We are passing down poorly lit walkways outside the building, among garbage bins and debris strewn across the pathways. P's flashlight points

TABLE 3.5
Reported public agency responses to properties secured by Intelligarde

Agency	n	%
Police	128	37.9
Ambulance	28	8.2
Fire	10	5.9
MTHA	2	.6

Based on systematic random sample (n = 340) of company occurrence report files (N = 1,703) (at 95% confidence interval, p = .05, precision = ±5%). MTHA = Metropolitan Toronto Housing Authority Security.

to another crack can.[19] I know how to recognize them by now. We talk briefly about double-spent matches[20] and the circus of 'welfare night.'

P: You should come back when they get their welfare cheques. This whole back area is covered with people lying around as high as a kite.

Me: When is that?

P: I think the end of the month is this Friday. You should come on the weekend. [Smiles] Man, if you want to see what we do, come back then.

Me: Where are we going now?

P: I've gotta check on things in this building ... You see those houses over there? We take care of all of them. You know, they know I'm coming but I don't bust them in exchange for information sometimes.

Me: What kind of information?

P: Anything. Who's coming, who's going, what they're selling.

Me: Shouldn't the cops be doing that?

P: They've got no time or they don't care. I know everybody here, and if I don't know them I ask questions. I get to know everybody. There isn't a cop in this city who knows more about who's dealing down here than I do. It's not bragging or anything, it's just the way it is.

We continue walking through a back alley and into the brightness of street lights. Only ten yards behind us is another world inhabited by 'crack heads' and dealers and policed by Intelligarde. We continue to another building with external balconies and a paved courtyard. The building is not a hospitable place. It is much too dark, and litter is scattered about the property. Graffiti is sprayed on most of the walls. I know I would not feel comfortable here alone.

P: On my third night at this site I had a B and E. Right there [*pointing*] on the third floor.

Me: What happened?

P: I saw him breaking in, I jumped into the hallway and pursued him. I called for back-up and three guys were coming. He came down here and they got him just outside the property and down the alleyway.

Me: How long did it take them to get here?

P: Oh, seconds. We've got about four guys in the area at any given time, not to mention mobile and PAT,[21] they like to hang around here too.

As we pass by a tattered and unlit Neighbourhood Watch sign, I begin to chuckle. I cannot believe that anything resembling a 'neighbourhood' or community could be said to exist here. I consult my meagre mental library on failed police attempts to construct artificial neighbourhoods and the lip service given to community rhetorics. I shake my head and continue laughing quietly as the sign vanishes in the darkness behind us.

P: What are you laughing at? Are you laughing at the sign?

Me: Yeah, actually. Is there actually anything like a community here? Do people really care?

P: You know something? When I found that guy breaking in, I found him because all these people were hanging off their balconies pointing at the guy. They were screaming. And when I lost him, they pointed him out again so I could tell back-up where he was going.

Me: You're kidding me.

P: Nope.

Me: But you said these people are all drugged up. You made it sound like that's all they do.

P: I meant it. I wouldn't go ten feet near some of these people if I didn't have to. I swear to you they can't even get up enough energy to walk their fucking dogs. You knock on their door and a wave of this smell of dog shit hits you. Most of them are doped up, alcoholics, or just MI.[22] They won't even open the fucking door. Animal control comes down here to take the dog and they can't get in. But you can smell the shit in the hallway. So then we have to take matters further through eviction ...

Me: So they helped you get the guy?

P: I didn't believe it myself. But here are all these losers, guys we've busted before screaming directions at me. It's almost as if you can do all the dope you want, and sell all the dope you want, but just don't rip anybody off ... [*Laughter*].

By now we have left the building and are crossing back toward the site I was originally dropped off at. P stops at another rooming house along the way. He asks a tenant an assortment of questions through a door he only barely opens. The tired older white man looks intoxicated. There is an odour.

P: Well.

Me: Well, what?

P: Didn't you fucking smell that!?

Me: Oh, yeah, it smelled like a toilet.

P: You mean shit. Are you not supposed to say that on tape? I just wanted to make sure you didn't think I was pulling your chain.

Me: How do you work in conditions like these?

P: Actually, this isn't so bad. This is a tolerable risk factor, but there's action. You can make this place as busy or as slow as you want. There's always going to be somebody doing something. If you don't do anything about it, no one's going to get hurt. Up at Kipling and Steeles it's different. If they say they're going to shoot you, they probably will. You have to take that sort of thing seriously. At least once per rotation we're threatened. You gotta make sure everybody knows about the threat and who made it.

Much like the public police, therefore, Intelligarde officers are able to 'make crime' in an environment of 'dependent uncertainty and boredom' (Ericson, 1982: 61–72). They sit on a veritable goldmine of potential arrests that can be harvested on a whim – to 'look busy,' to 'pump the stats,' or to alleviate boredom and create excitement. Obviously, this dynamic varies from site to site. Young gang members in western North York may be less willing to tolerate arbitrary arrests than older, drug-dependent tenants in downtown Toronto.

P decides to detour through one of the building's hallways. I notice a number of Deister[23] strips on the walls and door jambs and ask him why he is not striking them. He has already completed his patrol – this walkabout is purely for my benefit. As we pass down the second-floor hallway, P stops outside one of the doorways.

P: Do you hear that?
Me: Yeah, what are you going to do?

He does not answer but knocks repeatedly on the door. The music remains on, the volume constant. P makes a fist and bangs on the door: 'Security!' Finally, a lean, tall, young, shirtless black man answers the door. His eyes are glassy and bloodshot and he is angered by our presence. He looks either drunk or high.

Man: Too loud? [*Mumbling*]
P: Yeah, it's way past eleven, can you turn it down a bit?
Man: I respect what you gotta do. I do.
P: If you can just turn it down.

The man goes back into his room and turns down the music. We walk away, but P stops us only a few paces later. 'Wait a second,' he says. It sounds as if the man has turned the volume back up again, and P shakes his head in disappointment. He asks me to confirm that the music volume did go back up again. I tell him that I think it did, and quickly regret my honesty as P marches back to the door. I cringe as P begins knocking again.

Man: Still too loud? I need to unwind man. It's been a long day.
P: Yeah, but there are other people trying to sleep.
Man: Want me to turn it down?

The man stands at the doorway and sucks his teeth. He sways from side to side in an intimidating manner, dropping one shoulder and then the next as he moves toward P. He is not going to go back into his room. He walks out into the hallway and toward me. I fear he has mistaken me for a security agent.

Man: You want me to turn it down?
Me: [*Looking over at P*] Yes, please.
Man: Wait right here.

As the young man goes back into his apartment, I begin imagining every possible ensuing horror. I see my own demise. I envision him spinning out of the doorway with a machine gun, or an axe, or a knife, or a bat. I have watched far too many television crime dramas. My heart is pounding until I finally hear the music go down.

P: Thank you.
Me: Yes, thank you very much sir.
Man: I respect you. You got a job to do. [*Shakes my hand*]

As we walk toward the meeting place, I know I could never do this for a living. Just when I think my heart rate is back to normal, P stops outside a doorway to an apartment with the hinges removed. There are signs of forced entry, as the screws look as if they have been ripped from the frame. The door is resting on the jamb. P begins to knock, and a crackled female voice is heard in response.

P: Hello? Are you allright? Miss?
Woman: Oooh ...
P: [*To me*] I know this woman, she's a prostitute ... [*To the woman*] Are
            you OK?
Woman: [*Moaning*]
P: Can I come in? Are you all right?
Woman: Oh, just fuck off! I'm trying to get some fucking sleep.
P: What happened to the door, ma'am?
Woman: I dunno.
P: Do you know it's broken?
Woman: Fuck off!
P: [*Under his breath*] Fine, fuck you. [*To me*] I'll fill out a report on the
            door.

P makes notes in his booklet, and we move across well-lit city streets and back to the original site. In the lobby of the building we are met by M. A check by radio confirms that C is on his way. Some more gossip ensues. I am surprised that P reports none of our adventures to M while we are waiting, but I soon realize that nothing has actually happened. I begin to appreciate the routine terror that policing alone, without a dog and without a gun, might bring in this environment, and how important meetings with fellow security officers become. But these are my interpretations, and I want to test them with P, M, and C. I want to ask them how they feel about each other, the fear involved in their work, and the reliance they have on one another. I look forward to interviewing them independently in the next few weeks. C arrives.

C:	Let's do it.
M:	Are you ready for a trip through the sewer?
Me:	What do you mean?
P:	It's the underground parking area. We've got squatters. When was ...?
M:	It's about one week ago. We had people living down there. In the back entrance, actually. They live in the abandoned cars on the very bottom level.
Me:	Are they still there?
C:	Are they?
M:	No. I don't think so ... Did you hear what happened?
C:	With the rocks?
P:	Tell George.
M:	They threw rocks at us.
Me:	Rocks?
M:	Yeah, they brought rocks with them and started throwing at the s/o. [*Laughter*]

As we descend toward the lower levels it gets more difficult to breathe. The air is stagnant and filled with dust. There is dust everywhere. It cakes the concrete stairwells and the handrails and turns everything to grey. It is also very dark. All of the light bulbs have been broken, and there is nothing but a couple of flashlights to lead our way. M kicks open a sheet metal door and rummages through storage lockers. He finds some blankets and a burnt mattress. The security officers are all familiar with the mattress. We enter the parking level. It is so dark I can't see my hand in front of my face. As the flashlights turn toward abandoned cars, eerie shadows are cast, providing the illusion of movement. The cars are missing tires, have broken windows and missing doors, and are buried in close to a quarter-inch of grey dust.

Me:	I can't believe this is Toronto.
M:	Pretty bad, huh?

I am *trying* to be reflexive at this point about what we are doing. My sociological training tells me I am excited and apprehensive because I have vilified the squatters based on stories and unflattering narratives.[24] That does not change the fact that I would rather not be here. We eventually find an abandoned car with the dust wiped from the rear window. It is in the very far corner of the parking level, in complete darkness. M approaches the car and shines his flashlight through the passenger-side window. There is broken glass at his feet and garbage about the car. The security officers believe someone was recently using it as a home. M finds something – a pair of boots and a paper bag with a few tins of preserved food.

Me: What are you going to do now? [*With much apprehension*]
M: Nothing. I'm not going to take the guy's food if that's what you're worried about. If I see him here, I'll remove him. But I don't need any Spam, do you?

This chapter introduced the parapolice function as a crime control model and problematized popular assumptions about the role of the public and private police. Having reviewed the multiple and overlapping characteristics of the public and private police, we can now clearly appreciater the modern organization of commodified policing in risk markets. In addition, an examination of security officers' powers of arrest and the role of Intelligarde in exacting private justice further reveals the organization's law enforcement focus. A statistical comparison of the mobilizations of the MTP and Intelligarde International, as well as an ethnographic account of parapolicing, provide evidence of the commodified nature of law enforcement and the interchangeable logics of the public and private police. In the next chapter I examine the recruitment, employment, and training practices of The Law Enforcement Company as a precursor to a discussion of the politics of private contract security in risk markets.

FOUR

Inside a Law Enforcement Company

Intelligarde's advertising circular begins with a prosaic declaration of our times: 'Demand for policing is up. Police resources are down.' At the very outset, The Law Enforcement Company positions itself as an answer to citizen's fears and shrinking state security budgets:

> Every day our news media is full of reports of break-ins, vehicle theft, vandalism, fraud – the list goes on. More recently, crimes like carjackings and home invasions are becoming commonplace. Disorderly conduct and the drug culture threatens most neighbourhoods, in cities and towns alike.
>
> At the same time, budgets for police services are being drastically reduced. Responsibility for protection is being downloaded onto municipalities. The number of police officers available to answer calls for help is being cut.
>
> Result? An increasingly concerned and frustrated public is turning to private companies for the security services they so desperately need. Municipalities, business and property owners, institutions, corporations, and individuals are looking for reliable, affordable policing that can be tailored to suit their special requirements.
>
> This is where Intelligarde comes in. (Intelligarde, nd)

Since it was founded in 1982, the firm has grown steadily from an initial fleet of four cars and a dozen security officers to 20 cars and 150 staff. Intelligarde sells itself as an alternative to complete reliance on the public police. The circular promotes Intelligarde security personnel as top calibre, well trained, and highly skilled. Intelligarde considers its market advantage to be staff 'empowerment,' which in this context means that 'their up-to-date knowledge of the law and their high standard of training [prepares them to] take charge of the most challenging situations ... and make arrests when necessary.' To understand this competitive 'advantage,' we must assess the product being sold – the security officer – and the production process itself. In this chapter I explain how the firm recruits tests, trains, and initially deploys its officers. More importantly, I show how its new officers respond in practice to the processes. Having experienced all of the firm's selection and indoctrination procedures as an observer participant,[1] I offer observational data from actual testing and training sessions. Later in this chapter I take up the politically heated issues of race, class, and gender in the doing of parapolicing.

Recruitment

Prospective Intelligarde employees are drawn to the company by various means. Often, interested applicants learn about Intelligarde simply by spotting company vehicles around the city. The mere look of an Intelligarde officer or vehicle is enough to attract some applicants:

We get quite a few that way. They see the car. They like the car. They're like roving advertisements for people interested in law enforcement. (Intelligarde manager)

I saw a car drive by once and I called the number. I was already working with another security company, and I wanted to get involved with a company that wasn't Mickey Mouse. So I checked them out and liked what I saw and here I am. (mobile security officer – male)

Another recruitment tool is 'word of mouth' – personal contacts with current Intelligarde officers. One mobile security officer told me that he had personally recruited five friends from other security companies. Movement between security firms is common in the industry. Erickson (1993: 24, see Table 7) found that 51 per cent of licensed security guards in Toronto had worked for at least two companies in the past five years. At Intelligarde, 60 per cent of all uniformed staff (for whom such information existed in the personnel files, $n = 112$)[2] had worked previously for other firms in the security industry:

I heard about Intelligarde from a friend. He told me about the company and I thought I'd check it out. (mobile security officer – female)

Me and my buddies came over from Intertech. We all decided to give it a try.

This is nothing like any other security company, and I've worked for four different companies. (static site officer – male)

But the most common way to attract applicants is through local newspaper ads. Lately, this has been Intelligarde's option of choice:

I don't know why, but the calibre and even the quantity of available labour in the Toronto area in shrinking. I've been trying to get us to expand our search outside the GTA. (Intelligarde manager)

I came here through an ad in the paper. I needed a job ... Actually, my background is in the military. (static site officer – male)

More creative measures have also been employed. To promote the firm, senior Intelligarde officers responsible for staffing visit community colleges that offer programs in law and security or law enforcement. These programs vary significantly in quality, however, so Intelligarde staff have become more selective about which colleges they visit.

Erickson (1993: 27, see Table 9) found that 80 per cent of security guards in the GTA had been recruited through newspaper advertisements or personal contacts. Similarly, most of the officers I interviewed ($n = 40$) migrated to Intelligarde after hearing about the company's reputation. Often they had spoken to friends who had moved to the firm, or media coverage of Intelligarde had piqued their interest. While I was writing this book, the Canadian Broadcasting Corporation (CBC) broadcast a special program on private policing that focused on Intelligarde, and this resulted in a spurt of new applicants. More recently, Intelligarde has been recruiting from a shrinking labour market, and newspaper advertisements have become crucial to recruiting.

Pre-employment Testing

Anyone who is interested in becoming a security officer at Intelligarde International must fill out an application. If the paperwork looks attractive to Human Resources, the applicant is called in for an interview. Often the interview takes place at the time of application. Soon afterwards, the applicant is assigned to a training officer, signs a waiver, and embarks on a mandatory ride-along. This ride-along serves two purposes: it allows the training officer to assess the applicant in an actual job setting, and it allows the applicant to witness first-hand the job environment he or she will be thrust into. Prospective employees are always told that they will be returned to headquarters at any time if they feel this is not a job they wish to pursue. Most applicants bail out of the process after the ride-along.

I accompanied one prospective Intelligarde employee on a ride-along. The training officer begins the session by verifying that the waiver has been signed and that the applicant is aware of the evening's purpose. He tells the applicant that he will be evaluating her, but that at the same time she should be deciding whether she wants to continue with the training and hiring process. It seems that a training officer's main task is to expose applicants to the grittier components of parapolicing, and to dissuade them if they are skittish about the work.

Also assessed during the ride-along is the applicant's ability to write reports, hit Deisters, and take notes. The ability to produce information is crucial to security work. The applicant is told that her ability to write quickly and take notes will be assessed. The notes must follow a specific format that is identical to the one used by the public police. Heavy emphasis is also placed on a narrative reporting style. This is in sharp contrast to much of the report writing done by public police officers, who are typically asked to fill out forms replete with check boxes. These mobile inspection reports are left at the site for the landowner's perusal. No matter how good a security officer is at patrolling, handling crises, and making arrests, these will all be for nothing if his or her actions cannot be justified in a courtroom or successfully sold on the market. Representation is of paramount importance to parapolicing, so applicants are evaluated on their ability to generate a product that will be satisfactory to the client:

You've got to make nothing into something. Even though nothing happens on your patrol when you hit a site, you have to fill up the page. Writing 'nothing to report' is unacceptable. Something *did* happen. You must have seen something irregular. If not, then write where you went and what you did. (mobile security officer – male)

Training

As I enter the briefing room at Intelligarde headquarters, I see five young white men and one woman already seated. Most of the men have closely cropped hair. They are evenly spaced through the room, but no one sits at the front table. A few of them study me as I take a chair off to one side. I detect considerable tension. There is complete silence as they wait for their instructor. In an office adjacent to the briefing room, I see at least three hopefuls filling out applications. The applicants look in at the trainees as they complete their paperwork. I take out my tape recorder and place it on a filing cabinet beside me. No one is talking. My note taking is putting everyone on edge. I surmise that they must be thinking I am evaluating them, so I stop writing. Finally, two of the young men in the back row begin to chatter about the expected length of the course today. It is now past nine a.m., and we are getting restless.

An Intelligarde manager arrives by car. A few of the applicants look over. The briefing room is walled by large windows facing the lot and the car bays, so the recruits can easily monitor the comings and goings of staff. I suppose they are wondering who their instructor will be. A strong, stocky figure marches into the room. He is wearing a black Intelligarde uniform with utility belt, handcuff pouch, holster, and 9 mm semiautomatic handgun. He is animated when he speaks to me.

D: So, I guess you got approved. [*Smiles and shakes my hand*]. You should have gone out and got drunk!

The rest of the group is eyeing me suspiciously.

D: I was talking to a nice old lady the other day and she was comple-menting us on our appearance. She asked, 'Is that a real bulletproof vest?' I said, 'Yes ma'am, it is.' And then she says, 'It doesn't stick out like it does for the police.' [*He laughs, I smile*] We drink but we don't get fat.

The recruits are smiling. I know that D is using me as a foil while cleverly indoctrinating the group on the differences between the police and Intelligarde: they are old and fat, we are young and vital. I don't like being used, but D has immediately set the tone.

D: I don't know what kind of a group we've got here – they laugh like girls. [*Smiling*] We've got to look tough but we're nice guys.

Another recruit has joined us. There are now six men and one woman. Soon the four men in the back row begin to talk about their previous employment. They discuss security work at a Montreal casino, working for the government, and finally the possibility of doing armed escorts at

Maple Leaf Gardens. One of the recruits hopes he will see some hockey games while at Intelligarde. D begins the session, and everyone is given a training package. They will be tested throughout the course. The candidates are expected to complete reports during the course of this training session. They will hand them back at the end of today's session for evaluation.

D asks the candidates how they came to the company. Three of them answer that they responded to a newspaper ad. One says he saw the cars and decided to apply. Another cites 'word of mouth,' and another says he has a friend at Intelligarde. D takes advantage of this to explain to the candidates the differences between Intelligarde and the rest of the policing market.

D: We're not just another security company. No other security company
        compares to Intelligarde. We're not police either, and we're not try-
        ing to be the police. We are a private law enforcement company. We
        are ourselves ... The cops don't know what community policing is.
        They will either arrest or not. At Intelligarde we build a history and a
        case. We know our environment. We interact with the people daily.
        When a suspect vehicle – a drug car – is around you may be better
        off doing intelligence. Who is the tenant being visited? Do I know
        him? Why don't I know him?

The recruits are now taking notes and listening intently. This is what many of them came here to do – real law enforcement, real police work. They are being equipped right away with the organizational rhetorics they will need to argue back at Intelligarde's detractors. More specifically, they are being told quickly that they can do much more than the public police to maintain social order.

D: An Intelligarde officer can do much more than a cop in stopping a
        noise complaint. They have to rely on bylaws that are not very strict.
        You can blast your stereo until 11 o'clock in Toronto. That's just not
        acceptable. If somebody calls the police for a noise complaint in this
        city, guess what happens? Nothing. They don't show up. And if they
        do show up they'll take an hour. And when they do show up, they'll
        ask the tenant to turn it down and when the cops leave it will go
        right back up again. They have to rely on bylaws. We rely on contract
        law. They can lose their apartment much quicker if we're called. So
        you visit the complainant and make sure he knows you're on his

side. You empower him. Then you take care of the problem. And you go back again and again while on patrol.

This talk of private powers captivates the candidates. Many of them can hardly believe how much authority they will be able to exert on private property. They are told, 'As long as you can justify it, make the arrest.' Once D begins discussing the Trespass to Property Act, we all begin to understand the extraordinary powers of arrest enjoyed by security officers (see Chapter 3). Under s.2(1)(a)(ii), anybody can be arrested for any prohibited activity. D lists all of the possibilities under federal, provincial, and municipal laws.

D: We take the Trespass to Property Act as seriously as the police take the Criminal Code. The Trespass to Property Act is your best friend – treat it with respect.

This part of the training elicits many questions and 'what if' scenarios. D handles these patiently at first, before halting discussion later. There is much more material to cover.

D outlines the arrest process and the legal requirements faced by security officers. The candidates are told how to escalate detention to arrest. One must always attempt to avoid making an arrest, if possible, because this places legal onuses on the officer and the company. Instead, they should detain first and then, if the suspect attempts to flee, stand in his way. By this approach, less serious offences can be escalated into assault. He then begins discussing 'politically correct' terms to be used when writing reports and taking notes. The recruits are to write 'restraints' instead of handcuffs, and 'dark complexion' instead of negro, and so on. The race relations tutorial continues haphazardly.

D: You have to be aware of cultural differences. Sometimes you see garbage in the hallways or you might see garbage piled up in a garbage room right next to the chute. And you ask yourself, 'What's the matter with these people, are they fucking pigs?' Well, often they don't know any better. As silly as it may seem, they've never been shown how the garbage chute works. So sometimes you have to take them by the hand and show them. It's the same with these Sri Lankan women. Their toilet is overflowing and you realize it's because they're trying to flush tampons or diapers down the toilet. They've never seen a toilet before.

In response to a question from the candidates, D begins to discuss the uniform requirements. Everyone wants to know when and where they will get their uniforms. The candidates are upset to hear that the company will not pay for these, though it will help finance them, especially the bulletproof vests. Also, 80 per cent of outfitting expenses are recoverable through the federal government. D notes that Intelligarde has all the necessary paperwork for the application.

D: I'll give you the address and number of a place where you can get your handcuffs – it's where many of the guys go. You have to have your own personally tailored vest, and depending on how big you are, you're looking at around four hundred dollars. You will purchase a garrison and utility belt with six cheaters and a six-cell maglite flashlight. When you buy your handcuff pouch, you must make sure it is one that fully encloses over the handcuffs.

After hours of tutoring on report and notebook writing, time management, and company policies, the candidates are all given radios to practise their phonetic alphabets and radio codes. The briefing room comes alive with chirps and beeps as the students key their cellular radios. I take up a radio myself and soon realize that the buttons and digital window baffle me. Eventually I begin to understand the system, and am alarmed that there is no single communications frequency: you must key the specific officer or district you want and speak on a private channel. The same process is used to call the dispatchers, which means that only one officer can speak to headquarters at a time.[3] An officer who needs to call for help can scroll to the 'group call' channel, which overrides all other communications. We are told that this is an option of last resort and costs Intelligarde hundreds of dollars every time it is used. The radio system is confusing for the recruits and aggravating for seasoned officers. As I am to find out in upcoming interviews, the latter will invariably ridicule the communications system (see Chapter 5).

One of the last requirements of the day is a trip to the kennels. The candidates are eager to take a look at the dogs. We all walk over to two small structures housing over twenty dogs. The barking is deafening as we press into the small walkways separating the cages. This trip is harrowing for me. The dogs are lunging at us through the wired cage fronts. Dog training is an essential part of security provision at Intelligarde International. The firm's canine trainer, F, tells us that a dog is often worth five partners in subduing crowds and keeping a security officer safe. F is a grizzled and experienced veteran of security work. He will be responsible for initial canine training and for all subsequent training. The candidates ask many questions. Each security officer will be trained with two dogs: a primary and a back-up. And each security officer will be responsible for grooming and maintaining those two animals.

The next day of training covers self-defence and the tactical use of handcuffs. Everybody but the lone woman applicant is present. She will later resurface as communications officer. The trainees are eager to meet their instructor, as his reputation precedes him. Today he is close to an hour late. While we wait outside an inconspicuous garage, the discussion turns to previous employment. Everyone has stories to tell. Finally, the recruits ask me to call Intelligarde to find out what is keeping B. Nobody else feels comfortable enough to make the call, so I oblige. I return with the news that he is on his way and that we are to wait for him. When B arrives he is wearing athletic wear and carrying an assortment of pads. He apologizes for being late; apparently he was misinformed about the date. He also had to drop his daughter off at school.

We descend into a church basement. There are mats lining the floor and two flags, Portuguese and Canadian, on the far wall. B begins speaking, and everyone strains to hear. There is some construction under way upstairs. He gives his instructions:

B: Self-defence training is always ongoing. You should be coming back
        to keep sharp and continue learning. You must be in shape to be
        able to capture a suspect. There is always the possibility you could
        get hurt if you are not in shape. Your partner relies on your assis-
        tance. I'm sixty and I still work out and look after myself. It's up to
        you after this initial law enforcement self-defence.

B's audience is rapt. This is what most of the recruits have been waiting for – training on how to subdue a suspect, how to make a lawful arrest, how to be and act like a real police officer. B continues his introduction by emphasizing that all actions must be justifiable in court.

B: In law enforcement we counterpunch. We do not strike first ...
        Always step back from your opponent. Distance equals safety. You
        should remain at a forty-five degree angle to the person with your
        hands up – Especially the lead hand ... Mobility and stability.

By now everyone is beginning to understand that all actions must be defensible in a courtroom before a judge or jury. We have to assume that every movement we make may be used against us later. So B equips us with the vocabulary of law enforcement.

B: You have to speak the legal language of defence. Imagine yourself in a courtroom. We don't kick, we step forward. When he's down, we step forward to relax him ... we never say 'I kicked him into submission.' [*Smiles*]

The recruits laugh. Some of the trainees are having difficulty mastering some of the take-downs that B is demonstrating. He is patient, and continues with his tutorial on justifiable behaviour.

B: The bad guy can hit you anywhere he pleases, but we have restrictions, so aim for the central body mass. No head shots because it makes for lousy pictures. Besides, people can take head shots, and the head is hard to hit. Do not strike for the kidneys, kneecaps, groin, throat, or neck area. Aim for the stomach. You try to wind him with no serious physical effects.

B teaches the trainees how to make a fist and throw a punch. The first two knuckles are to be used. The recruits begin to experiment with the various techniques, mixing and embellishing them. Their actions become more feverish when the punching pads are introduced. B begins to instruct them on the correct way to deliver a kick. By now the trainees are working up a sweat, and most of them are panting. There are melees under way in all parts of the makeshift gymnasium. Now B brings forward boxing gloves. I surmise that hours of sparring must improve confidence. The recruits seem to be enjoying themselves. After this, the trainees are instructed on how to search suspects.

B: As a private citizen, you cannot search for identification. You are empowered to look for weapons or tools that may aid in his escape ... Ask for consent. If you find something, play stupid until you receive consent. Now anything you find can be used in evidence. If you find drugs, leave them for the police.

Eventually B begins to instruct the students on proper handcuffing procedure:

B: Grab for the elbow to control the bad guy. Do not force a reaction. Once he cooperates, reward him with less pain.

He tells the class that while this basic handcuffing information is mandatory, later training in advanced handcuffing techniques is not. However,
all Intelligarde officers are encouraged to enrol for the extra training.

B: The law is your tool – like a mechanic. If you know the law, you can
            better do your job. If I don't have him under this section, I'll use
            another one ... I'll place a guy under arrest for littering so that I can
            get his name.

Intelligarde's chief trainer draws from a deep fund of anecdotes to
entrance his audience. He cites cases where suspects were charged
under obscure sections of the Environmental Protection Act. In one,
they were charged with shaking cigarette ashes onto a public sidewalk;
in another, they were arrested on suspicion of picking worms in the
park after dark. The point was always to make them identify themselves
so that interrogation could begin.

As we break for lunch, B tells me that the level of legal training the
recruits are receiving is slipping. They still have too many questions by
the time they come to him for physical training. As a trainer of security
officers, he has a special appreciation for the private side of law enforcement. The class retires to a nearby delicatessen. At the deli the trainees
exchange more stories about previous security and fight experience.
They discuss powers of arrest and exchange anecdotes and information
they may have pulled together about Intelligarde. B pulls up a chair and
asks me about the research. I do my best to answer. I devise my own
hypothetical arrest situations to clarify my understanding of the law on
private property. He responds to them thoughtfully. It is clear that B is
well respected by his students. After years with Intelligarde, he has
trained hundreds of security guards both at the entry level and at more
advanced stages.

When we return to the gym, B revisits the Trespass to Property Act.
The class is confused. I decide to return to Intelligarde headquarters,
and wish the group well. After today, each of the trainees will undergo
three nights of site exposure and hours of canine instruction. Some will
go directly to mobile patrol, but most will start at static sites. Mobile
patrol is considered a prestige appointment, and managers tend to
reserve it for proven security officers or exceptional neophytes.

Rookies

New Intelligarde officers can place a great deal of stress on existing
social networks. The term 'cherry' reflects a masculinist perception of

untested employees – that they are inherently virginal until they have proven themselves to the rest of their platoon. Rookie security officers present a number of challenges to the rank and file because no one is sure of their character or readiness for duty. This is magnified if the new officer is assigned to mobile patrol:

The worst thing they can do is when they put someone on mobile who doesn't know what they're doing. We rely on mobile for back-up. In some places there's no one around except the closest car. It's happened before where a car from across the city got to the scene first because the new officer did not know where the site was. That's totally fucking unacceptable. (static site officer – male)

There's no point putting someone in mobile who doesn't know where all the sites are. They train them on that, but sometimes they get transferred into a new district and then we're in trouble. Everybody has to keep on top of that and help out. (mobile security officer – male)

But this fear that a new security officer won't be able to find his way to aid his colleagues only begins to explain the reservations that seasoned guards have about 'cherries.' An even more common fear is that new security officers will be overzealous, and sabotage years of relations with tenants at a given site:

Up here in the west end things are rough. They can be pretty scary sometimes. We can't have some gung-ho guys trying to kick heads every night. If somebody's doing that my life gets harder. If I have to run to help out some new guy all the time, I'm running into danger. (static site officer – male)

When this guy comes around here and thinks he's going to make a name for himself and I'm supposed to cover his fucking ass, that pisses me off. We don't need people like that, and I do what I can to get rid of them quickly. Because if I don't, it could be my life. Many times they see the uniform, they see that I'm alone, and I could end up paying for his stupidity. (static site officer – male)

Rookie security officers may compromise a state of social order that has taken months or even years to establish. So veteran officers are nervous until they are comfortable that their new partners understand the threshold of tolerance at a given location. Quite often, security officers who do not seem to be functioning well at a given site are transferred to another at the request of more senior officers. Managers take these assessments seriously, as a new officer's overzealousness could easily lead to violence.

A final source of concern is rookies who are women. Intelligarde has been receiving more applications from women. Many seasoned officers were reluctant to critize the women they were working with, but their body language and gestures clearly indicated displeasure. Respondents would role their eyes and say 'next question,' or would simply offer a 'no comment.' Some officers were less reserved:

What are they good for? I mean, I'm not a sexist or anything, but what the hell is a female going to do if I need back-up? What if she's the first one on the scene? It's not like we have guns or anything, so I mean ... you tell me, what are they good for? (static site officer – male)

Well, thank goodness there's not that many of them. I don't have any personal grudge against women doing police work. It's just that if I need assistance I want a very, very big man to help me. (mobile security officer – male)

I agree that if I'm in a jam I would also want a guy to back me up. But then again, I don't plan on getting into jams. The guys who end up in brawls are usually the guys looking for it. I don't look for it ... Well, then yeah, if you put it that way and I had to choose, I'd say I'd want the police or a bunch of guys to come running, but that's a loaded question. (mobile security officer – female)

So long as they do their Deisters and don't cry wolf, everybody's happy. I mean, I'm friends with them. I'm just not going to call them, and frankly I don't think they *want* to be called. (mobile security officer – male)

These comments reflect not only attitudes toward new female officers, but also general subcultural attitudes toward women in police work. I will say more about this later.

Who Are the Parapolice?

Intelligarde officers are trained in powers of arrest, legal note taking, and self-defence, and usually have some college law enforcement training. This is not the norm for the security industry. Shearing, Farnell, and Stenning (1980: 157) found that only 43 per cent of security guards had undergone any training on the legal powers of arrest for security officers; Erickson thirteen years later (1993: 30) found this figure to be

TABLE 4.1
The average Intelligarde security officer

Characteristics	Median†
Sex	Male
Age	25
Complexion	White
Height	5'11"
Weight	180 lbs.
Education	Some college
Major	Law & security related
Service with Intelligarde	16 months
Previous security experience	6 months

†Population varies ($n = 96$ to 141) depending upon missing data.
Based on employee personnel files ($N = 141$).

57 per cent. Similarly, Erickson (1993: 30) found that only 58 per cent of security officers had received instruction on note-taking techniques.

At Intelligarde, self-defence training is a standard one-day course, with extensive additional training thereafter; yet Erickson (1993: 18) found that only 38 per cent of security officers in Toronto reported that they had received any self-defence instruction. More importantly, Erickson also found (1993: 30) that only 15 per cent of those who had undergone defence training had received that training at their present employer. Either a few security companies are offering self-defence training in an industry with a nomadic employee base, or many security officers enrol in martial arts training on their own. Surprisingly, more and more security employees are taking college courses in law enforcement or security. In Erickson's study (1993: 18), 42 per cent of respondents reported some related college training; yet close to 70 per cent of Intelligarde officers are currently enrolled in or have completed law enforcement or criminal justice training. The overall number of contract security guards with postsecondary diplomas increased between 1980 and 1993 from 10 per cent (Shearing, Farnell, and Stenning, 1980: 140) to 47 per cent (Erickson, 1993: 16); yet 67 per cent of Intelligarde staff have college diplomas or university degrees or have almost completed them. Almost 10 per cent of Intelligarde security officers have been to university. The typical Intelligarde officer is a young, white male with some college training in law enforcement or security and just under two years of security experience (see Table 4.1). Erickson (1993:

15) found that 34 per cent of security guards in Toronto were women; however, this is not reflected at Intelligarde, where the staff is 92 per cent male. This may be because of the dangerous nature of the security work that Intelligarde does (see Chapter 3), or the macho culture this cultivates (Chapter 6), or general recruiting practices. Erickson (1993: 22 [8 per cent]) and Shearing, Farnell, and Stenning (1980: 150 [3 per cent]) found that very few security officers had a background in public policing. This also holds true for Intelligarde officers (see Table 4.2).

The average age of an Intelligarde officer is 26.2, which is significantly lower than the industry norm. It is also lower than the mean age for uniformed officers in the local public police, which is 38.7 (Metropolitan Toronto Police Service, 1995b). Shearing, Farnell, and Stenning found in 1980 that 65 per cent of security guards in Ontario were over 30; in 1993, Erickson (1993: 15) observed that the mean age of security officers in Toronto was 37. There are other differences besides these between Intelligarde officers and the rest of the security industry. The percentage of Canadian-born security officers employed by contract firms has dropped in recent decades, from 57 per cent in 1980 (Shearing, Farnell and Stenning, 1980: 141) to 44 per cent in 1993 (Erickson, 1993: 15). In contrast, 77 per cent of Intelligarde staff were born in Canada – a far higher percentage than in the rest of the industry. The second most common country of birth for Intelligarde staff is Jamaica (4 per cent). The reputation and recruiting of Intelligarde International has resulted in a well-educated, male, young, white labour force specifically seeking opportunities to carry out the type of law enforcement activities that Intelligarde does. So in support of Intelligarde's promotional rhetorics, the company does differ significantly from the industry standard.

Race, Class, Gender

Fear, the demand for security, and the need to minimize risk cannot be divorced from race, class, and gender. Barely hidden by the cold rhetorics of actuarialism is a layer of emotion that is actually counterintuitive to instrumental logics. This only fuels further calculation, collation and the purchase of security products. Risk markets are not cold, calculated, rational terrains – this is only their representational form. In the following section I expose the more base (or 'classic') ingredients for the mobilization of security.

Intelligarde is used to accusations of racism levelled by both tenants and the media. The idea of private stormtroopers harassing young black

TABLE 4.2
Composition of uniformed Intelligarde security staff

Characteristics		*n*	%
Sex (*N* = 141)	Male	130	92.2
	Female	11	7.8
Age (*N* = 123)	<19	3	2.4
	20–25	69	56.1
	26–31	32	26.0
	32–37	12	9.8
	38–43	3	2.4
	>43	4	3.3
Complexion/race† (*N* = 134)	White	102	76.1
	Black	13	9.7
	Hispanic/olive/med.	9	6.7
	East Indian	9	6.7
	Asian	1	.7
Education (*N* = 138)	High school	45	32.6
	College	80	58.0
	University	13	9.4
College or university major (*N* = 93)	Law enfor. or crim.	66	68.7
	Other	30	31.3
Citizenship (*N* = 132)	Canadian	123	93.2
	Other	9	6.8
Licence (*N* = 141)	Security guard	118	83.7
	Dual (+PI)	23	16.3
Military or police exp. (*N* = 123)	None	95	77.2
	Military	24	19.5
	Military police	2	1.6
	Police	2	1.6
Offences (*N* = 126)	None	119	94.4
	One or more	7	5.6
Residency (*N* = 133)	Outside GTA	33	24.8
	Within GTA	100	75.2
	Toronto	49	36.8
	Scarborough	16	12.0
	Mississauga	12	9.0
	Etobicoke/Rexdale/Weston	6	4.5
	East York	6	4.5
	York	6	4.5
	North York	5	3.8

Based on employee personnel files (*N* = 141). GTA = Greater Toronto Area, PI = private investigator, †based on employee self-report item on application for security guard and/or PI licensing men prompts images of 'Soweto-style' oppression (*Toronto Star*, 11 August 1993: A7). The realities of racism in police and criminal justice practices have been well documented in the criminological literature (e.g., DeKeseredy and MacLean, 1990; Lynch and Patterson, 1990; Reiman, 1995). In August 1993, Intelligarde raised the ire of newspaper journalists as a result of its activities at an affordable-housing complex at Toronto's harbourfront:

> They've called off the dogs in the Bathurst Quay Cityhome complex. But not the privately hired security guards who chase black kids through the neighbourhood, harass visitors walking their girlfriends back home, threaten residents with eviction, and browbeat their way through the community making citizen's arrests. (*Toronto Star*, 11 August 1993: A7)

> Jake seethes with resentment at the security guards. 'Last month, I was riding my bike from the park. I stopped for a minute on the Cityhome property. These two guards jump me, throw me to the ground, slap handcuffs on me. I get away and I start to run. They chase me, with their dogs, all the way over to the Tip-Top building. So now they've got me cornered and one of them says: "Don't move nigger, we've got the cops with us." Hey, I was glad to see the cops. They took me down to 14 Division. Got a ticket for trespassing and they let me go.' (*Toronto Star*, 13 August 1993: A7)

Cleverly, the columnist questioned the motives of the tenants who had requested Intelligarde's presence, arguing that their fears were racially motivated:

> To be sure, many – probably most – community residents would agree with McLeod. They supported the security blitz, want the dogs back, and are anxious to get those loitering kids out of sight and out of mind. But when you ask these trembling tenants what, in fact, is so threatening, so objectionable, about the youths' behaviour, the answers are vague and unsatisfying. 'I've seen them drinking in the park,' offers one woman. Golly. But their resentment, their fear, their silly little acts of urban espionage, none of this has to do with the fact that these idling teens are black, does it? (*Toronto Star*, 13 August 1993: A7)

After this episode, Cityhome's acting director sent a letter of reprimand to Intelligarde management requesting that the officers merely observe and report wrongdoings instead of making arrests. Intelligarde, in need of positive public relations, hired black activist Dudley Laws to school the officers at the Cityhome property in question. When Laws was reported to be under the 'employ' of Intelligarde, the *Toronto Star* was forced to publish a correction:

> Black activist Dudley Laws has been invited to deliver a lecture on racial sensitivity, for a $150 fee, to Intelligarde International Inc. security who work at the Bathurst Quay complex, but is not on the payroll of Intelligarde International Inc. as a story implied. (*Toronto Star*, 23 August 1993: A3)

Clearly, Laws wanted to distance himself from an organization that was publicly perceived to be racist in its policing practices.

There is very little doubt that residential buildings tenanted mainly by blacks pose a particular policing problem for Intelligarde staff. Residents' affiliations often extend into 'gang' memberships; even more commonly, however, they reflect loosely organized coalitions of convenience in the face of perceived racist threats.[4] While this tension often exists before Intelligarde's arrival, it can be exacerbated by the presence of overzealous security officers. As I patrolled the corridors and exterior of a North York apartment building with three Intelligarde security officers, we passed by inflammatory graffiti: 'All niggers must die!' 'Security pigs can kiss my purple ass!' The latter message was sprayed on the building's rear outside wall in foot-high lettering.

More recently, the company was the subject of allegations of racism and beating up on the poor. On 24 May 1996 a black tenant of 200 Sherbourne Street – an Intelligarde-secured property – was allegedly tackled, beaten, and kicked by two of the company's officers. As it often does, Intelligarde processed the case through a private information to a justice of the peace. The black man, Roger Carr, claimed that he had been beaten by the security officers. The incident had been captured on videotape and was eventually released to the television media. This was a public relations disaster for the company. The judge assigned to the case, Mr Justice Porter, eventually ruled that the incident was precipitated by Carr when he returned to the lobby security cage with a coat hanger:

> The lobby is covered to a limited degree by a video camera. Counsel agree and I concur that the video is not perfect, but it is helpful. It shows, and I find, an agitated Carr at the bars of the cage, which is in keeping with the

evidence of the guards. It also shows Huyton leaving the cage and Carr approaching him, in what I consider an aggressive fashion, with a coathanger in hand[5]

Judge Porter went on to find that Huyton had been defending himself in taking Carr to the floor, and that when Carr resisted, another security officer had come to assist. The charges were dismissed, with the judge noting: 'There is no doubt that Carr suffered injuries, but I find that he was the author of his own misfortune.'[6] This case is further evidence of Intelligarde's poor reputation among many in the communities they protect.

The Ontario Coalition Against Poverty (OCAP) has mounted a campaign of protest against what it perceives as 'Intelligarde's assault on the poor' (OCAP, 8 May 1997). It has organized protest rallies and circulated pamphlets and posters in support of Carr: 'The Carr case was a focal point for us but we know that once the heat is off, Intelligarde will resume their heavy-handed extremes. Sooner or later there will be another situation' (John Clarke – Provincial organizer, personal communication, 12 March 1998).

OCAP's protests against Intelligarde are the only ones targeting a 'private' company. The coalition's organizers concede that Intelligarde has no monopoly on violence against the poor but add that the firm's officers do their work with such zeal that they stand alone in comparison to both MTHA security and the MTP. OCAP cites several incidents in which Intelligarde officers used excessive force. In one, a man was visiting a friend at a nearby Cityhome property when he was arrested for trespassing by Intelligarde security officers and banned from all Cityhome properties. A problem arose when it was discovered that the trespasser was a Cityhome resident of another building – in effect, he had been banned from entering his own apartment.

Have Intelligarde officers displayed racist attitudes? Have their mobilizations been racially motivated? To some extent, this has been the case. Intelligarde's own managers invited Dudley Laws to lecture their officers, and it has been alleged that some Intelligarde officers have directed racial slurs at black suspects. Despite my diligence in this regard, I did not find any overt racism in the attitudes of security officers. However, I did witness two incidents in which Intelligarde officers seemed overzealous and confrontational with black suspects.

I am interviewing two Intelligarde officers at a security office in a North York apartment building when a mobile officer arrives to report that there are 'a couple of black guys drinking in their car outside.' The youngest officer leaps to his feet and reaches for his radio. Four other officers also begin collecting themselves for a confrontation. I immediately wonder why everyone is getting so excited, especially considering that there have recently been physical battles between the security officers and black tenants. Why would we want to start something? The officers run out into the hallway and through the lobby to the roadway key in front of the building, and find three young black men in a white sports car. It is after 11 p.m. and it is raining.

S/O 1:   Are you drinking? You can't have an open drink in the car. You're under arrest.
Driver: Oh man, what's your problem?
Pass 1:   You're not police. You ain't no fucking police!
S/O 2:   Get out of the car!
Pass 2:   Fuck you, man. You can't arrest us.
Pass 1:   What the fuck. [*punching seat*] You can't arrest us!
S/O 3:   [*To me*] This is what I mean when I say some guys take it too far. You should stand up against the building because people will start throwing stuff down on us. Somebody threw a couch on one of our cars once. But they might throw bottles or knives. You should get out of the way.
Me: Here?
S/O 3:   Yeah, good.

After some grappling through the driver's side window, the young men drive off. I question the security officers about why they decided to attempt an arrest. One confides that they 'looked dangerous.' Another says that 'the law is the law.' I ask why they didn't simply call the police, and they have no real answer. This is their turf, and since the incident did not escalate into a serious one, police assistance was not necessary. The security officers are adamant that the youths were engaged in prohibited activity on private property and that they could therefore be arrested. I wonder whether the same tactics would have been used had the young men been white.

    The intersection of race and class (Schwartz and Milovanovic, 1996; Messerschmidt, 1997) is a topic of some interest in criminology's theoretical discourse. Most researchers concede that there are surely overlaps between racism and poverty; some privilege class ahead of, or as a function of, race (Reiman, 1995). This debate need not concern us here. It suffices to assert that racism and poverty are often linked, especially as it affects Intelligarde's contacts with the populations it is tasked with controlling.

One Intelligarde officer relates how his actions came into conflict with a homeless man.

C: I'll tell you about this one time I was at the Greyhound bus station. Well, we took over the contract from another security company that ... I don't know, I guess none of them did anything. So, I'm on patrol and I come across this sleeper in one of the stairwells, you know, in an area where people can walk by all the time. So I tell him he has to go and he goes crazy.

Me: He attacked you?

C: No, nothing like that. He just couldn't believe we were telling him to leave. He was angry. You know, he's thinking, 'This is my home, *you* get out.'

Me: Did he leave?

C: Oh yeah, sure. But the point is that the guy was living there for something like two years. It's like I walked into your home and told you to get out. I don't think you'd want to leave.

Me: Nobody had said anything?

C: I guess none of the other security guards from the other crappy companies ever told the guy, or made him leave. The old guy had set up shop, he had his little radio there, and blankets and food ... The thing is, they must have had to step around him to do their patrols. [*Laughs*] Unbelievable.

Intelligarde has involved itself in charitable work for the homeless. In February 1996, Intelligarde teamed up with the Canadian military and the St John patrol in what was called Operation Cold Snap. While soldiers staffed the warm-up area inside Moss Park Armoury, Intelligarde patrol officers picked up any homeless people they found, along with St John Ambulance personnel (*Toronto Star*, 5 February 1996: A6). The community pitched in by donating, sweaters, sleeping bags, candles, coffee, doughnuts, and pots of stew (*Toronto Star*, 6 February 1996: A2). The operation received considerable play in the media, and Intelligarde's efforts were mentioned in Toronto's largest daily newspaper:

Intelligarde International security officers, who are contracted to patrol housing complexes, public buildings and transportation systems, have

TABLE 4.3
Residency reports of persons issued notices prohibiting entry†

Residency‡	N	%
Gave address	1543	59.0
No fixed address	917	35.0
Unknown, blank, refused	157	6.0
Totals	2617	100

†Based on one-year sampling (August 1996–September 1997, N = 2617) of Intelligarde bannings database.
‡Item entered by security officer on notice prohibiting
entry.

made a commitment to check on people huddled outside. They are offering any takers a ride to the armoury, and are giving out candles provided
by Acadian Candle Co. to those who won't come. (6 February 1996: A2)

Some Intelligarde staff defined the operation as simply 'good PR.' The
officers themselves wanted me to know that it was a ploy for public support – something that would let management argue later that they were
actively engaged in helping the homeless even while they were evicting
them from company sites.

With the Carr case, newspaper reports, and the OCAP protests in
mind, I decided to examine more closely Intelligarde's deployment and
training practices. If the company really was prejudiced toward the populations under its purview, surely these attitudes would manifest themselves both structurally, in its internal politics, and publicly, in its arrest
reports. I applied the same test for gender discrimination – a topic that I
will address more systematically later in this section. First of all, there is
little doubt that Intelligarde polices the most economically disadvan-
taged populations in the GTA. This is clear from the statistics compiled
from NPEs. When one collapses individuals who reported having no
fixed address with those who would not divulge their residency or for
whom no information was listed, one finds that 41 per cent of the people
who have been banned from properties policed by Intelligarde are
homeless (see Table 4.3). Some additional things are worth noting here.
First, there is no statistically significant difference for residency between
males and females issued NPEs (χ^2 = 2.012, df = 2, p = ns). There is, however, a statistically significant difference with regard to residency

between banned individuals on the basis of race (χ^2 = 65.350, df = 10, $p <$ .001, not shown).[7] This difference is especially noticeable among banned Native people, 63.4 per cent (n = 45) of whom reported having no fixed address. In comparison, reported homelessness among whites, Hispanics/South Americans, blacks, and East Indians ranged between 23.7 and 37.9 per cent. Only 7 Asians (9.5 per cent) reported having no fixed address to return to. Another queer statistical finding is that the mean age of banned males and females also varies significantly (t = 6.465, df = 1189.174, $p <$ .001, not shown): 31.8 for men, but 28.6 for women. I do not know why such a variance should exist, especially when one considers that the mean age for women banned from Intelligarde properties for prostitution is 31.9. This should raise the overall average age for women, since they monopolized that NPE category. Instead, there is an overall trend across all NPE categories showing that women are younger than men; this also translates into an aggregate difference. General Canadian crime data, however, repeatedly indicate that women mature out of deviancy and criminal activity more quickly than men (Juristat, 1999). These latter findings, however interesting, have little to do with assessing whether Intelligarde's mobilizations indicate prejudice.

Most people banned from Intelligarde properties by NPEs are reportedly white (63.9 per cent), while just over one in five are black (21.4 per cent). The remainder of banned individuals are described as having a 'medium' complexion (5.4 per cent), or are believed to be of East Indian (3.1 per cent), Asian (3.1 per cent), or Native (2.1 per cent) descent. Even if we knew how closely this banned population[8] (n = 2,406) reflected actual Intelligarde-secured populations, we would still not be able to discern bias in policing. This is because many of the individuals banned from Intelligarde properties are obviously not tenants. It would be unfair for us to compare NPE issuances against the general population, because members of ethnic minority groups often interact socially with members of their own community. In other words, there is no guarantee that the people visiting and/or intruding on Intelligarde properties reflect the general population of Toronto. No completely defensible conclusions can be culled from such an approach, because we can't ascertain a justifiable comparison (or base) population without long-term systematic observation of Intelligarde-secured lobbies and properties.

Considering all this, it is worth looking at how Intelligarde deploys its visible minority and female officers. The first observation we might make is that Intelligarde is three times more likely than the public

TABLE 4.4
The relationship between employee demographics and job training

Employee demographics

Training	Male (N = 129)	Female (N = 11)	X- value† df = 1	White (N = 102)	Visible others‡ (N = 32)	X- value† df = 1
Baton	3.9	0	.442	2.9	0	.963
Dog	53.5	27.3	2.789	53.9	34.4	3.723
Gun	45.0	9.1	5.349*	44.1	28.1	2.589
MLEO	23.8	0	3.362	23.5	9.4	3.033

*p < .05, † all Pearson X-square calculations based on 2 × 2 table (df = 1), ‡ based on employee self-report item on application for security guard and/or PI licensing. Numbers presented in percentages. MLEO = municipal law enf. officer (parking).

police to hire visible minorities – 7.6 per cent of uniformed MTP officers belong to these groups (Metropolitan Toronto Police Service, 1998: form #c-3.1) compared to 23.9 per cent for Intelligarde. Intelligarde does not do as well when it comes to gender: 11.2 per cent of police officers in Toronto are women, but only 7.8 per cent of Intelligarde staff (see Table 4.2).

When we scrutinize Intelligarde's training practices, we find no statistically significant differences for either race or gender, except that women are much less likely to be certified for handguns (see Table 4.4). Across all other training qualifications – including MLEO, dog handling, and baton licensing – there are no significant differences. Visible minorities and women are less likely to be trained across all additional (i.e., beyond standard training) aspects of security work compared to their white male counterparts, though this is not statistically significant. The fact that female security officers are far less likely to be qualified for handguns may be a product of gender role socialization, or management's reluctance to involve them, or both. This modest statistical indicator of race and gender bias in training extends to *deployment* for race only. In other words, in statistical terms, white security officers are significantly more likely to be deployed in mobile patrol than their minority counterparts (see Table 4.5).[9] This is a provocative finding, because mobile patrol is considered a prestige appointment. This result holds true even when we consider the presence of possible differences in the employee pool between white and nonwhite security officers. For

TABLE 4.5
The relationship between employee demographics and job placement

Employee demographics

Placement	Male (N = 128)	Female (N = 9)	X-value† df = 1	White (N = 100)	Visible others‡ (N = 32)	X-value† df = 1
Mobile	25.0	27.3	.028	30.0	12.5	3.882*
Static/comm.	75.0	72.7		70.0	87.5	

*p < .05, † all Pearson X-square calculations based on 2 × 2 table (df = 1), ‡ based on employee self-report item on application for security guard and/or PI licensing.

instance, when comparing factors such as age ($t = .164$, df = 118, p = ns), education ($t = .596$, df = 132, p = ns), previous security experience ($t = .501$, df = 107, p = ns), and service to the company ($t = .692$, df = 128, p = ns) – factors that might otherwise explain differences in career advancement – we find no statistically significant difference between white and visible minority security officers. Absent employee preferences, therefore, one must conclude that assignment to either a mobile or static security function can be attributed to extra-meritorious factors such as race.

When I put these results to Intelligarde middle managers, they responded that they weren't biased, and that the differences I had found were a function of 'individual motivations' (for training) and job success (for placement into mobile patrol). I had half-expected them to argue that deployments reflected company needs – that is, a deliberate decision to deploy minority officers at sites when minorities were more prevalent, so that fewer were available for mobile duty. This, I was assured, was not the case.

Intelligarde officers who are members of visible minority groups reported no overt discrimination against them in the company. Some, however, did note a much more subtle process that transcended overt actions. In any case, black officers in particular reported that they are forced by the occupation and by the populations they police to confront 'working for the man.' One black officer noted:

Some of these Jamaican guys, they suck their teeth to disrespect you, but that stuff don't bother me. These guys call me 'roast breadfruit' sometimes. It means white on the inside, black on the outside. Like an Oreo, you know? But I don't let that stuff get to me. (static site officer – male)

Women, on the other hand, did not hesitate to voice their concerns about an unpleasant working environment:

A couple of guys, one guy in particular, was spreading rumours about me in the company. He was saying that I was a slut. It got back to me and I dealt with it. I confronted him about it and made him stop. (mobile security officer – female)

You always have to watch yourself because many of these guys don't think you should be here. I'm trying to make it into the police force and so are most of these guys. They already have negative attitudes toward female officers. (mobile security officer – female)

Macho subcultures, like those of the police, do not provide hospitable environments for women (Rigakos, 1995; Smith and Gray, 1983). As men test their masculinity against one another (see Messerschmidt, 1993), they must repeatedly reconstitute their bravado. One of the methods employed involves objectifying, sexualizing or diminishing women.

The doing of security work at Intelligarde is also the doing of 'gender' (Newburn and Stanko, 1994). In other words, being a man is a social action that requires consistent reassertion. Messerschmidt (1997) asserts that masculinity is stratified, in the sense that more affluent men are more masculine than poorer men, and heterosexual men are more masculine than homosexual men. Thus, while Intelligarde security officers may be less masculine than the public police because they lack peace officer status and are considered 'wannabes,' they are still men, after all, and can assert their masculinity against women. In any work environment dominated by men, women will be perceived as devaluing the cultural status of that organization by weakening its claim to universal masculinity.

At Intelligarde, this dynamic often showed itself in casual banter and briefing room discussions. With a female trainee present in the briefing room for her first ride-along, an Intelligarde training officer asked why another woman was being assigned to a dangerous site:

You know what's going to happen, don't you? The call will come over the radio, 'Help me, I'm being raped.' [Laughter]

Thus, on her first day of interaction with Intelligarde, the applicant was made aware that female security officers are not thought of highly at the company.

Security officers preparing for shift work often looked out into the walkway to assess the attractiveness of any female applicant in the lobby. Typically they would comment on her physique and the sexual activities they would like to engage in with her. Any female security officers who were present would simply ignore their comments. But the bias extended further than this – it was systematic.

Female security officers are not assigned to dangerous districts unless absolutely necessary, and do not usually patrol high-risk sites unless partnered with a male security officer. There is also a heavy bias toward placing women on day shift to 'avoid difficulties.' Female officers are well aware of their situation:

I have to work twice as hard as the male does to earn respect. To prove myself. I've been here for a month and I'm already mobile and the only reason is because they need more women out in the public eye. I wasn't moved into mobile because I was good or had something special to offer. It was just the sort of thing where they needed more women so I have to work twice as hard to prove myself. (mobile security officer – female)

Another female security officer seemed grateful that she was not being thrust into more dangerous situations:

I'm not here to get killed. I'm here to get a paycheque, and I'm happy doing what I'm doing ... Sure, I worry if I get moved to another shift or district. (mobile security officer – female)

Erickson, Albanese, and Drakulic (2000) have found that gender-role determination in the Toronto security industry can be variable. Women often find enhanced opportunities to engage in managerial and/or covert security operations. These assignments reflect the possibility for women to engage in gender-atypical work. On the other hand, the authors also find that there is still resistance to women engaging in uniform-related or physical security work. This resistance is exaggerated and amplified in Intelligarde's macho occupational culture. Whether it is motivated by the dangerous realities of parapolicing among Toronto's lumpenproletariat, or a sexist understanding of women's limitations in hostile environments, or a paternalistic – indeed, chivalrous – attitude toward protecting women, Intelligarde treats its female security officers differently than it does its male employees.

In the next chapter, I describe how Intelligarde actually does surveillance and control, and how these systems are sold on the security market.

FIVE

A Parapolice Surveillance System

Tasking private police forces with controlling 'unruly' populations is not a new phenomenon. Since the private Marine police of the Thames River, under the direction of the early police scientist Patrick Colquhoun, such organizations were required to engage in the minutiae of public and private order (McMullan, 1998: 105–6). The Marine police of 1800 enforced rules of conduct and monitored the river's proletariat, by implementing dress codes, paying 'lumping rates,' managing accounting, determining wagelessness, and stopping illegal activities on London's shipping lane. They prevented losses and apprehended thieves by applying themselves to the apparent trivialities of order maintenance: no frocks, wide trousers, jemmies, or hidden pockets were allowed on board boats, and any on-the-job takings were forbidden and confiscated: 'Surveillance thus becomes a decisive economic operator both as an internal part of the production machinery and as a specific mechanism in the disciplinary power' (Foucault, 1977: 175).

The police came to 'know' their populations by categorizing and administering them. Colquhoun (1800, as cited in McMullan, 1998: 108) and other police intellectuals (e.g., Chadwick) developed classification systems the purpose of which was to transform transient masses into known populations that could be counted and managed. Factory discipline, prison administration, poor houses, child support, and public health and sanitation were all part of the base of a strategically erected pyramidic hierarchy aimed at pastorizing the poor. All networks were incorporated into an elaborate, top-down state program.

Modern private police organizations ply their business under different social and structural conditions. While there is little doubt that workplace populations require monitoring, surveillance is embedded in the matrix of doing business: in the technology of producing and in the very act of movement. To a lesser extent, this involves the same policing dynamic as was found in early nineteenth-century England: outsiders must be monitored as potential threats, as illegitimate interlopers in the legitimate pursuit of profit. But nowadays they are electronically tagged (Lyon, 1994: 102), and their movements regulated by means of a laby- rinth of technological passkeys and recognition systems. The raison d'être of systems like this has remained largely unchanged since the 1600s (Rigakos and Hadden, 2001). Access is determined by risk catego- rization at the moment of contact with the production system. The vast majority of modern security revolves around loss prevention and access control – liberal economic rhetorics that are ideologically insidious because they are profoundly depoliticizing. Within the system, confron- tation is bypassed – the key either fits the lock or it does not. In either case access is a product of your classification, and your stamping is suffi- cient to warrant official disinterest until a blatant violation has occurred. This is the world of 'snowflakes'[1] (Shearing and Stenning, 1982b) as apparatuses in a network of fluid inaccessibility, in which culpability is diffused among both offender and victim (Shearing, 2000). Under cor- porate logics, both parties are to blame for the loss of hardware, time, manpower, and, ultimately and most importantly, profits. The institution knows that security precautions (such as target hardening) are central to minimizing risk and therefore loss – in this actuarial fantasy, the two are definitionally interlinked. This is the major part, and the overarching ideological mobilizer, of the modern dominion of private security.

But parapolicing has merged the loss prevention impetus of fluid access control systems with the gritty chaos of street-level law enforce- ment: it is just as much about retribution as it is about loss prevention. Private security officers are not imagined as professionals – at least not in the sense of having ultimate accountability and an independent occu- pational code. But even if they were, this would not make them immune from constant examination or free them from procedural constraints, as is purportedly the case with doctors (Castel, 1991) and public police officers (Ericson and Haggerty, 1997). Like their proletarian brothers, security guards and watchmen have historically been poorly paid wage labourers who are perceived as needing constant scrutiny. Like the fac- tory worker, who punches a time clock under the watchful eye of the owner and his 'police,' the security agent is required to make his where- abouts known: he must punch a mobile card mounted to a clock dial saddled over his shoulders at stations placed intermittently throughout the plant. The indentations left on the card are later scrutinized and the guards' whereabouts known. The watcher is also watched.

Perpetual Examination

The means of correct training (Foucault, 1977: 170–94) for security personnel ensure that they will monitor vigilantly the populations they have been assigned: white or blue collar workers, tenants, the homeless, prisoners, detainees, and courtroom personnel. Knowing immediately (telematicism), or knowing 'in advance' of the occurrence, is part of the fantasy of the new 'police machine' (Bogard, 1996). Actuarialism and the art of prediction combine to form the epistemological backdrop that makes this apparition possible within the logic of modern governance. It is a fiction; even so, it powers apparatuses of social control, in contest with the populations it is meant to ensnare. In this complex system of relationships, the state's monopoly over control is replaced by a constellation of interests, at once contractually and economically at variance and in alliance – by a spectre of control embedded in a nuanced system of unobtrusive management, safety, and risk management systems, all of these amplified by technologies of surveillance. How do the parapolice become 'known' while producing knowledge about others? How is surveillance of the parapolice carried out? More importantly, how are these techniques sold as a commodity?

I have already established that Intelligarde International is not representative of the general market for contract private security. Perhaps, however, its parapolice are harbingers of a new order in the private management of populations – a new order the specific purpose of which is to address (late) modern angst and fear of crime and disorder, and to fill the vacuum left by the retreating state (Rose, 1996). Intelligarde is as interested in *crime* prevention as it is in *loss* prevention, and its mobilizations are testimony to this. The parapolice of Intelligarde are not confined to the smooth surfaces and calculated access points of the modern security-industrial[2] installation; rather, they have been charged with organizing the chaos of public housing developments, the transient populations of rooming houses, the drug-addicted prostitutes of Cabbagetown, and the 'gang bangers' of North York. The site and context of private security surveillance has thus radically reverted to its early modern manifestations. The private security industry first began to grow rapidly when giant corporations began to acquire massive amounts of private property (Shearing and Stenning, 1983). The territories that security firms are now hired to secure are dispersed, fragmented, and have multiple owners albeit with similar security problems. In these chaotic environments, there is no state-of-the-art access control, and no tangible sense of community, and only limited informal face-to-face accountability. Into such environments steps Intelligarde International. Each episode of chaos is an opportunity for management, for risk eradication, for the purchase of comfort, and for the ideological dispersal of mistrust and fear. The firm must establish a system of surveillance and order maintenance that disciplines its security officers and that monitors and 'makes known' the populations it has been hired to manage. Even more important, it must find ways to sell this system on the open risk market.

Intelligarde has accomplished all of this in multiple ways. Foucault (1977: 184–94) suggests that examination involves establishing a discipline that is highly ritualized, ceremonious, and intrusive. Over time, this process is normalized within the routine of management. It becomes perpetual, unobtrusive, and devoid of its previous regalia. This is not to say that ceremonial examination entirely disappears, but it does mean that as the techniques of management are 'perfected,' the examination ceremony becomes little more than an adjunct to everyday and more routinized surveillance systems. As mechanisms of examination become embedded in the process of information production (Lyon, 1994; Poster, 1990), 'closing the gap' between the body of doctors, or soldiers – or in this case security officers – becomes paramount:

The briefing serves many purposes. It keeps everyone up to date about problem areas or tenants – it's an information-sharing opportunity. It also acts as an opportunity to set problems straight. If guys are slacking off, we can deal with it right there. (Intelligarde manager)

Uninterrupted processes of surveillance are now embedded in the imagination of all risk-reducing organizations and institutions (Dandeker, 1990). Surveillance is an obsession for security firms, since it is so important to their risk-reducing mandate. To establish perpetual surveillance, Intelligarde uses an electronic monitoring system that 'wires' the disordered spaces of Toronto's outsider populations and hooks these territories into the circuitry of ordered and accountable society. The process is based on documentation and virtual ordering. All Intelligarde-secured buildings are virtually mapped. Each site is first visited by Intelligarde managers, who affix 'Deister' strips[3] at a number of strategic points within and outside the property: on door frames, roof access points, underground parking supports, the insides of fire hose cabinets, and any other spaces frequented by 'sleepers' or 'druggies' or others posing a possible risk. Fire hose cabinets are notorious stash points for drugs, so to minimize corporate liability, security officers report misuse of fire equipment and poorly charged fire extinguishers. In large outdoor areas such as Toronto's harbourfront, strips are even attached to the backs of public road signs and railings. These strips contain bar code data and numeric digits, which are linked to a 'Deister' database. Each Intelligarde security officer carries a Deister gun similar to though much smaller than the universal price code readers used by supermarket cashiers. As the security officer conducts patrols, he scans the Deister strips; later, back at headquarters, he downloads this information into a computer.

Each Intelligarde mobile officer carries a small portfolio of Deister strips, which represent various happenings: arrests made, calls for PRO support (see below), investigations of drug activity or solicitation, reports of defective lights or abandoned vehicles, and so on. These 'portable' strips increase accountability and improve documentation, and allow the company's inspectorate to quickly glean why a particular patrol took longer than scheduled. Each incident matches a coded checkbox on Intelligarde's occurrence reports. Deister reports do not replace the paperwork; rather, they collate to the official digital incident. There are even Deister strips inside each security officer's portfolio to account for time spent writing reports in support of electronic records.

The challenge for Intelligarde managers is how to order the world of satellite problems with satellite employees. They meet it by manufacturing a virtual city of patrol checkpoints and digitally prefigured occurrences. Inside this virtual matrix, all actions consist of closed-ended, precoded outcomes within a computer-mediated system of total surveillance. The radio communications system provides a similar control mechanism – a process of perpetual accountability. Mobile patrol officers, and site officers at specific locations, are required to radio incidents to headquarters. Once they have, the communications officer can mobilize appropriate responses. Thus, there is a hierarchy of communication that fosters centralized decision-making based on a centralized pool of information. There are no communal or open lines (except in dire emergencies) – the new Mike system only allows for one-to-one cellular communications, most often between dispatch and line officers. Security officers are advised to keep their radios tuned to dispatch at all times, in case immediate assistance is needed, rather than to district or neighbouring security officers. This carefully structured isolationism is a product of management's need to cultivate a dependent and responsive (Manning, 1996) employee body. It also eliminates wasted single-frequency open communications between security guards – an action that often results in communications officers having to wait their turn in the information dissemination process. Within these alternate communications parameters, the hierarchy might be flattened, opened up, and transparent to other security personnel, allowing them to make proactive decisions on the basis of this candid information flow. Instead, a concentrated information hub manages the movements of dociled officers on the basis of organizational procedure. Ostensibly, this cuts out all 'other' units from the decision-making process, and bypasses unofficial or unsanctioned mobilizations.

The examination system also extends to more antiquated techniques. Security officers are scrutinized for the cleanliness of their vehicles, the maintenance of their dogs, and the condition of their uniforms. Paperwork is filed on each of these. Mobile security officers report that there is very little room for deviation from the uniform code. One security officer was disciplined in front of his co-workers for wearing an undershirt with coloured lettering that was visible through his Intelligarde work shirt. Reportedly, the officer was humiliated by his superior and ordered to either remove the undershirt immediately or turn it inside out. Another security officer was castigated for not wearing a tie during a hot afternoon in the autumn. One training officer reported that a security officer was summarily dismissed for failing to wear a tie after 1 October. Intelligarde policies clearly stipulate when ties become optional. Security officers often try to hide the provincially legislated 'security guard' lettering above the front pocket of their shirts with a tag book, a notebook, or an NPE book:

I see what these guys try to do sometimes with the notebooks. They try to disguise the words 'security guard,' but we do not tolerate that. The first time you're given a warning, the second time you're fired. I don't put up with that. We are a law enforcement company – we do not flout the law ourselves. I understand their motivations, but we are legally licensed as security guards and have to abide by the law. (Intelligarde manager)

Security officers who wear bulletproof vests or stab armour over their shirts must sew on a 'security guard' patch so that the public can easily read it.

Perpetual examination is a sometimes formalized, often inconspicuous form of power that requires repetition, uniformity, and consistency: 'Disciplinary punishment is, in the main, isomorphic with obligation to itself; it is not so much the vengeance of an outraged law as its repetition, in reduplicated insistence. So much so that corrective effect expected of it involves only incidental expiation and repentance; it is obtained directly through the mechanics of training. To punish is to exercise' (Foucault, 1977: 180).

Hierarchical structure is yet another mode of correct training in the sense that it establishes privilege and a role model system. In an attempt to improve the qualities of its security officers, the firm has established a distribution system in which officers are ranked by skills, aptitudes, and experience. Under this regime, Intelligarde supervisors are the 'best of the best' – they have internalized company logics and have been made responsible for ensuring an effective guard force. As one Intelligarde manager put it: 'We're looking for company men.'

Intelligarde has co-opted subcultural priorities and made them part of the regimented system. The company's problem resolution officer (PRO) competition consists of timed push-ups, sit-ups, and runs, and follows a regimented application system that closely mirrors that of the public police. Officers who pass the PROs are *de facto* capable of passing public police tests and are considered prime candidates for recruitment. Within a 'wannabe culture' (see Chapter 6), this status is respected. Security officers strive for professional and well-paying careers in public law enforcement; their direct superiors already have the physical skills necessary for this and are ostensibly well on their way to fulfilling their vocation. Thus, the PROs are closer to meeting the specific career goals of security officers, and at the same time are simultaneously regarded by Intelligarde executives as the best in the company. This new PRO program was implemented after five supervisors were dismissed or reassigned for failing to uphold company rhetorics and policies.

PROs are clearly different from other security officers. With their distinctive uniforms – black shirts and tactical pants with cargo pockets – they look more like militaristic SWAT team members than security officers. Not coincidentally, public police officers consider such tactical teams a prestige posting. The PRO embodies the quintessential police professional in appearance, qualifications, and mission, and at the same time reinforces Intelligarde policies. When finally assigned to patrol, the

PRO can take on various duties, including district watch, inspections of other security officers, special assignments, and back-up of fellow security personnel. It is a freelance position that involves trouble-shooting and encouraging other officers to comply with organizational schemas.

The final component of examination – the ordering of populations under company jurisdiction – is perhaps the most important. Much like their counterparts in the public police, the parapolice must make sense of an often chaotic work environment and produce knowledge of persons within their scope of intervention (Dandeker, 1990; Ericson, 1994; Marx and Reichman, 1987). They do this in order to establish a 'paper trail' for the purpose of justifying banishments or arrests:

The database does a couple of important things. It allows officers to immediately check a perp's history with us, it lets us know if this guy has been doing whatever he's been doing repeatedly so we can tell the police that when they arrive, and it lets the officers know if the guy is dangerous. Often many of the guys we have records on, the police have warrants outstanding against them. We may arrest them on one thing but the police want them for something else. (Intelligarde manager)

Intelligarde has compiled a database on all individuals against whom NPEs have been filed. Notices that have been issued against trespassers are filed with headquarters, along with shift reports and other paperwork. As part of their regular duties, daytime communications officers feed this information into the bannings database. The Law Enforcement Company dispenses thousands of NPEs and maintains an electronic case history of all individuals its officers have confronted. The NPEs contain more than just the names, addresses, and offences of banned individuals. They also include the specifics of the offence, including the date and time; the exact section of the Trespass to Property Act enforced; precisely where the offence occurred (i.e., in which stairwell or hallway); and details of the offender's appearance. This latter information includes height, weight, hair colour, hairstyle, attire, skin complexion, possible ethnicity, tattoos, and markings, and whether the offender was wearing glasses. Much of a parapolice officer's time is spent interacting with the homeless; as a result, Intelligarde has compiled Toronto's most comprehensive electronic registry of illegal or unofficial residences. These are the stairwells, alleys, and underground parking lots of the megacity. Much like Colquhoun's Marine Police of nineteenth-century London, the Law Enforcement Company has accumulated information about the movements and particulars of a city's underclass: who they are, where they are, what they do. Unlike the Thames police, Intelligarde, like other late modern observation institutions, has benefited from the power of computerization:

> Computers differ from other machines because they possess 'memory' and because they can 'talk' with each other using telecommunications ... It does enable human beings to do more easily many tasks that require brainwork. Unlike the machines of early industrialism, which multiplied musclepower, computers can be programmed to perform functions associated with mental power. (Lyon, 1994: 46)

Sociologists continue to ask themselves whether these new technologies have changed the nature of surveillance. Some argue that computers have done so qualitatively (Marx, 1988: 208); others doubt this but are still intrigued by the impact of computers (Lyon, 1994: 53–5). Certainly, because it is now possible to know populations almost immediately merely by conducting a simple database search, nets of surveillance have been widened (Cohen, 1985).

In one year (August 1996 to September 1997), Intelligarde personnel submitted approximately 56,400 written reports, ranging in importance from major occurrence reports to simple shift summaries and alarm responses. In this sense, 'knowing' involves remembering previous incidents and interactions. This is accomplished through a centralized computer system not unlike that of public police systems such as CPIC. Intelligarde has long considered hiring a permanent 'crime analyst' to collate and structure the piles of information filed by security officers daily.[4] When the information gathered starts to govern actual mobilizations instead of simply recording them, the new 'parapolice machine' will rival the public police in the use of surveillance technology. The act of information collection will then be part of the process of informed decision making through the use of actuarial logics.

Ericson and Haggerty (1997: 84) believe that the very act of information gathering *is* knowledge production, and that this, therefore, makes the police officer a knowledge broker. Even without secondary analysis – that is, reflection, collation, and argumentation – information is considered knowledge because it is organized in prescribed institutional formats. It serves the knowledge requirements of the institution. We might therefore conclude that the parapolice are also knowledge brokers. Indeed, the electronic bannings database often dictates security officer's actions based on the immediate retrieval of case histories. Should a suspect be arrested? Escorted from the property? Issued an NPE? The answers to these questions are mediated by a radio call to a communications officer, who enters the suspect's name (or other particulars) into a digital search field. The result of that query governs the action then taken. However, this process represents a very small number of mobilizations and is only initiated at the security officer's discretion. The occurrence files, alarm reports, and shift summaries are used mainly to discipline security work and assess its quality, or occasionally to answer client queries. Security officers undoubtedly navigate a digitally Taylorized workplace that produces streams of data about their own activities, but it is unclear whether this information, and information about the movements of the populations they are charged with monitoring, constitutes knowledge production. In the end, if information *is* knowledge, then what is information? But this need not cloud the more important observation that the parapolice are part of a structured, digitized, and perpetually scrutinized crime control company that observes not only the populations it is charged with monitoring but also those it employs to monitor them.

Hyperpanoptic Fantasies

Ever since Foucault (1977) examined the Benthamite prison, there has been considerable discussion and scholarship about panoptic surveillance. The idea of constructing all-seeing, all-knowing architectures of observation has been extended into the digital fabrics of modern social existence (e.g., Lyon, 1994). Panoptic surveillance has been employed as a metaphor for the general social control apparatuses of state and corporate institutions. Poster (1990) has argued that 'superpanopticons' consisting of digital information networks produce routine knowledge of populations within a social ordering increasingly contingent on information and communication. In this sense, the panoptic architecture is virtual. It does not have a physical presence; rather, it amasses *information* about populations and individuals, and does so with exponentially more success.

In Bogard's analysis of telematicism and surveillance (1996), the panoptic metaphor is extended further to a *panoptic imaginary*. In other words, the system of surveillance is one in which the goal is to know everything, immediately and at all times – and eventually even before it happens. This is theoretically possible in a landscape that is a simulacrum of some now only *relatively* important reality. If the task of technology is to construct its own more impressive virtual order, which is actually more real than the reality it was meant to represent, then the gap between reality and simulation becomes meaningless (cf. Baudrillard, 1983). In the end, the technologies of the present are simply a step toward the ultimate virtual order of hyperpanopticism. It is this imaginary future that Bogard seeks to theorize: 'Instead of architectures of control, walls and floors and viewing locations, we need to talk about cyberarchitectures, digital structures, and environments; instead of orderings of space and time, virtual space-times and coding conventions for displaying them onscreen; instead of visibilities and temporal series, about virtual light, programmed images, and cyberloops' (Bogard, 1996: 19).

I do not intend to take a similar ontological leap (see Rigakos, 1998); even so, Bogard's description of a hyperpanopticism with its fantasy of control, is highly useful when it comes to understanding what Intelligarde does. We need not entangle ourselves with epistemological pitfalls to make use of Bogard's thought on the fiction of total control.

To begin with, the Taylorized and panoptic workplace of Intelligarde International is obvious to most who enter it. The architecture of the compound makes the visual monitoring of security personnel effortless. The office of the company's inspectorate is right beside the car bays and is organized so that the quality control manager (QCM) has an unimpeded view of the comings and goings of security personnel. West of the office, right across from the communications room, is an open doorway onto the main corridor. If security officers report late for duty, management knows right away. It is here that mobile Intelligarde security officers must report at the beginning and end of their shifts to pick up their run sheets, report forms, Deister guns, site keys, radios and two batteries. All of this material is signed for by the security officer; a record is then logged by the communications officer, whose job it is to hand out workplace equipment. All of the equipment must, of course, be returned at shift's end. The security officers accept their daily assignments through a large window that separates the corridor from the communications centre. This design is very similar to that of a police duty desk.

On the east wall of the QCM's office is a door to the briefing room. This antechamber configuration makes it easy for the QCM to prepare his summaries and present himself to the platoon. Typically, the QCM prints out the Deister readings onto perforated computer paper in his office, and lays out the results across the tables in the briefing room.

Thus, the security officers are not only assessed and briefed before beginning their shifts, but also forced to reckon with their previous night's performance. Platoon tallies are posted regularly so that the different shifts can hardly avoid comparing their relative 'production' rates. The point of this is to foster competition among officers – that is, to inspire them to hit as many Deister checkpoints as possible. Security employees are made aware that they are always being examined, both physically and digitally, within a hyperpanoptic architecture that consistently seeks to 'close the gap' between the workers within its purview. Management can raise questions about elongated patrols, missed hits, and other disciplinary concerns that come to its attention through run sheets, reports, Deister readings, and client or tenant complaints.

One of the only places where a group of Intelligarde security officers can converse is in the briefing room just after they sign in but before the supervisor's presentation. Security officers who want to complain or commiserate must consider that their conversations can easily be heard by the QCM in the adjacent office. This is why there is often whispering in and around Intelligarde headquarters. On one occasion, as I was trying to conduct an interview, a security officer discreetly signalled that he would rather speak to me later. He gestured to the QCM's office. Another time, a training officer tried to complain to a fellow mobile security officer that he was being unfairly demoted. His colleague mumbled, 'That's your business, I don't want to hear about it' but soon after murmured 'later' under his breath. The same demoted training officer indicated that he wanted to talk to me in the washroom, but nonetheless *whispered* his complaints when I accompanied him there.

The QCM's office also has a panoptic view of the car bays, where all mobile security officers prepare for duty (see Figures 5.1 and 5.2). This position is symbolic, but also allows the QCM to watch security officers prepare their vehicles for the road. The care and maintenance of vehicles is of great concern to the company, since they are crucial to its operations. The supervisor takes this opportunity to ritualistically re-establish the company's hierarchy and bond with employees:

I sat here one time and watched this one guy spend close to half an hour cleaning the car because the fucking shitheads before him left it like a pig sty. The stuff just accumulates and finally this guy decides that this car needs a good cleaning inside and out. And I know the guy is a good officer. It's not his fault the car is the way it is. Now this is cutting into his shift and he has to rush around to get his run completed. So I decide that I'll help him out. I felt sorry for him. I

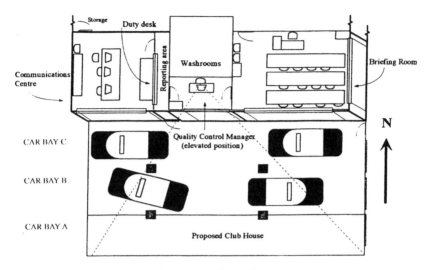

Figure 5.1   Intelligarde headquarters – floor plan

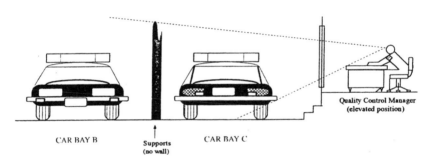

Figure 5.2   Intelligarde headquarters – cross-section showing elevation

helped him and other guys wash their cars. It's a form of socialization. (Intelligarde manager)

This notion of 'socialization' and bonding meshes structurally with the dominion of surveillance that the Law Enforcement Company imagines – in this latter case to oversee even proper leisure activity.

As I was completing my research, an officers' club was being established. Contractors had been notified, estimates had been submitted, the location had been decided on, the financing had been negotiated, and an officers' club management board had been formed. This club was not management's idea. It began with the employees showing an interest in fostering professional solidarity. Perhaps even more important, it would also be a convenient place for physical training. The two mobile security officers whose idea the club was were tired of paying exorbitant fitness club fees; they wanted to establish an organization similar to a police association, but without the political or unionist coloration:

This is not a union, it's a club. Like a military officers' club. It's a place to meet, talk, and relax without having to always make arrangements to go out somewhere. (mobile security officer – male)

It's an association of sorts, but it's not a union, and I think that maybe R was afraid of that when we first came up with it, but no, it isn't, and don't let him hear you calling it that. (mobile security officer – male)

Intelligarde agreed soon enough to deduct membership fees from the paycheques of those who joined the club, and also to contribute to the purchase of equipment and to donate a car bay for the structure.

   Not surprisingly, Intelligarde management had its own reasons for supporting an officers' club:

I'm excited by it and want to be involved with it. We want a management member on the board ... It'll be an excellent facility allowing for *structured socializing* ... this club will be a constructive way to socialize ... Spotting, for example – that develops trust among security officers ... These guys probably don't even recognize the potential. (Intelligarde manager; emphasis added)

Structured socializing, then, is a company imperative, similar to the imperative to discipline workers that arose around the same time as alienated production. Except here the hyperpanoptic gaze extends physically into the workers' leisure activities and developing occupational ethics. This opportunity fell into the lap of Intelligarde managers; even so, once it had, they grabbed the opportunity to control a productive form of socializing that they would be able to scrutinize. As matters were arranged, the club would fail without the company's cooperation on space, funding, and payroll deductions. Not coincidentally, the planned clubhouse is directly opposite the QCM's office. This meshes perfectly with the panoptic architecture of the facility (see Figure 5.1).

When the facility is completed, the company will be able to monitor both the work and the play of its employees without any effort.

The notion of hyperpanopticism, of course, is meant to transcend the physical spaces of observation as delineated by Bentham. The communications and monitoring systems of today are harbingers of a future system in which total control will be possible (Bogard, 1996). These digital and virtual orderings are in their infancy at Intelligarde, but they are coming in force, and the company's disciplinary techniques reflect the assumption that the future lies in embracing these orderings. Today, when a security officer is dispatched to an alarm call, the necessary information is transmitted digitally from a computer console at Intelligarde headquarters to a display window on his Mike radio system. The patrol officer responds to the page by radio, indicating that he has received the message and when he expects to arrive. The communications officer inputs the address of the alarm into a mapping software program provided by Perly's and transmits a map book page number and coordinates to the mobile security officer. The officer then checks his own Perly's map book and the coordinates, and sets off after the alarm. Quite often, communications officers 'talk' mobile security officers directly to a specified alarm location by maintaining communication with them as they travel cross streets toward the address.

This system has its problems. For example, the communications officer is not always certain where the closest security officer is located. Also, security officers are often on patrol in underground parking areas, in which case the page either cannot be sent or must wait for many minutes in a cellular transmission cue. Furthermore, an officer in neighbouring district may be in a better position to respond to an alarm that is in the same district. Of course, the security officer is expected to arrive at the scene of the alarm within thirty minutes; if he doesn't, he will have to explain himself in writing by issuing a 30-minute-plus alarm response report.

Intelligarde management is considering the purchase of a GPD (global positioning device) system capable of tracking the location of all units in the megacity of Toronto. GPDs would be affixed to all vehicles so that their whereabouts would be known to within a few feet. The entire mobile security force would thus be under perpetual surveillance by the communications centre computer. This is less a hyperpanoptic fantasy than an inevitability, given the tone of management's testimonials:

I'd really like to see, you know, and it's a strong possibility we'll be moving into GPDs, especially for our more inactive vehicles that have considerable down time. I would favour entirely splitting alarm response from mobile patrol duties to save costs and then going with the GPDs. (Intelligarde manager)

I like the GPDs. If hooked into the cars, it'll measure location but also acceleration, deceleration, and how many times the engine has been turned on or off. And by the way, this technology is now becoming affordable. I'd like to see it cheaper, but it can do some exceptional things. Another thing we have problems with is that some guys don't like to use their dogs on patrol. The dog gets taken out and then sits in the back of the car for the entire shift. We can hook the GPD into the doors of the cars so that we know if the dog's been taken out at that site. (Intelligarde manager)

Under a GPD system, all pertinent status information will be telematic, from the location of the security officer, to the distance to his next destination, to the mileage and speed of his vehicle. Also, all occurrences will be registered digitally. The communications officer will be able to tap this constant flow of information to make deployment decisions based on a virtual landscape of parapolicing mobilizations; order will thereby be found on a quintessentially chaotic reality. But for the hyperpanoptic eye, this is only the beginning: the same regimes of surveillance that make the security officer's world transparent will also be used to track the work habits of client companies' employees throughout the country and around the world.

Selling Surveillance in Risk Markets

Fundamentally, a parapolicing surveillance system is a management system for hire: a risk-reducing, profit-securing virtual network organized around the premise that residential and commercial territories can be ordered. Seen in this light, risk reduction is a contractual arrangement whereby residences are made liveable and factories are made profitable. Loss prevention and crime prevention have interchangeable logics and mechanisms of compliance. An essential goal for Intelligarde is to find ways to market a hyperpanoptic, Taylorized work environment for hire. To this end, it must find ways to demonstrate that it has internalized late modern actuarial practices for securing profits and people. While exerting control, it amasses information on the populations it is charged with monitoring, and also disciplines those populations. This makes the parapolice closer to the original idea of 'police' than their public competitors.

I have already noted that Intelligarde's electronic compendium of

Toronto's underclass rivals anything compiled by the city's various policing and social service agencies. But it cannot make any profit from this
amassed information unless its clients believe that such information is
key to its efforts to secure hostile and chaotic spaces. When selling security in late modern risk markets, it is an enormous advantage to be able
to make your security staff endlessly accountable to the clients who indirectly employ them. Neoliberal logics dictate that citizens are consumers
(Miller and Rose, 1997) and that historic state monopolies such as policing are now simply products to be bought and sold under free market
principles. The buyers of this product include not only large landowners
and corporations but also community groups and private citizens:

> One of the reasons we're flourishing is because people do not get redress. They
> don't feel their police are answerable to them – not just corporate Canada but
> the little guy. Residents' and tenants' associations demand service. The facile
> assumption that we work for the rich is patently false. Look at our clients – City-
> home, the Parking Authority, TEDCO – they're all municipal bodies where the
> little people are the end users, and they enjoy the most advanced security service
> in the city. (Intelligarde manager)

One way that consumers are guaranteed that their police will be
accountable to them is through Intelligarde's Deister system.

The Deister system is a metaphor for the selling of policing services in
late modern risk markets. It is ironic that Deister strips are fashioned
after universal price code stickers: the act of striking such surfaces
announces clearly its commodified nature. Clients are routinely sup-
plied Deister read-outs along with their invoices. This billing practice is
akin to providing the purchaser with an inventory of products being
bought, but it actually represents the internal digital surveillance system
of the company. The two are thus interchangeable – clients want to purchase total control and total accountability, and the Law Enforcement
Company sets about providing these. The keys here for Marxist thinking
are the unavoidable drive to accelerate dependence on technology and
the push to reinvent unproductive labour as 'productive' (Marx, 1975:
55). The increasing development of machinery to replace manual
labour hardly needs to be discussed here (but consider the development of CCTV, remote alarm monitoring, etc.). As well, it is a general
law of Marxian economics that unproductive labour (which produces
no material commodity and no surplus value) must somehow be made
to at least appear productive (Mandel, 1975). This is not the place, how-

ever, to offer a digression on Marxist economic law.[5] Suffice it to say that according to Marx, unproductive labour must at some point be trans- muted so as to begin producing material commodities. The next imag- inable step, of course, is to place the bar code on the security officer and the readers in the building. In this system, surveillance *is* a commodity.

Clients also want these systems in place for the purpose of minimizing liability. Now there will be irrefutable evidence that a security officer was in the building, that patrols were made, or that the said occurrence could not have happened as reported because the security officer was 'in that hallway at the time.' All of this is clearly recorded on the Deister read-out. In this way the management of risks is ingrained into the pro- cess of selling surveillance – it is the product. Of course, the digital sur- veillance system can also minimize liability for Intelligarde. On one occasion, Deister read-outs were presented to a justice of the peace as evidence that a security officer could not have been involved in an assault because he was in another part of the city.

For a hyperpanoptic private policing institution, the next logical step is to sell its wares to the public at large, in direct competition with the public police. In Ontario, since the provincial neoconservatives under Premier Mike Harris made changes to the Police Services Act, it has been possible for municipalities to contract for policing services through alter- native agencies. In the new municipality of Quinte West, Intelligarde was invited to enter a bid for policing services alongside the Trenton police and the OPP. During his presentation, Intelligarde president Ross McLeod held up the latest gadget in security officer surveillance equip- ment – a baton that would replace the aging, DOS-driven Deister system. Throughout, he used the prop to punctuate his central message: finan- cial and quality control over the local police service. If only five of the six officers assigned to a shift in a given night reported for duty, the munic- ipality would be refunded the cost of the missing officer. Squarely within the dictums of neoliberal risk eradication, consumers would pay only for the immediate surveillance they received. 'Can the public police prom- ise you that?' he asked. Given the nature of police unionism, the answer is of course obvious.

The Quinte West police board, much like the average Intelligarde cli- ent today, would receive a print-out of the mobilizations of each security officer. Electronic checkpoints would be placed outside and inside mer- chants' storefronts, on public road signs, and at problem areas such as schools and parking lots. The police board would have direct control over its officers without the political distance of a provincial police service situated at Queen's Park or the legal autonomy of the Trenton police. While placards outside demanded 'local control' and the continued presence of the Trenton police; inside, McLeod was introducing the newly constituted police consumer to the future of total control and total accountability under the direction of his hyperpanoptic organization. This was the ultimate so far in the evolution of police resource control and management:

With all of this talk of professionalism and detachment, the public has lost control. The cops say, 'Don't ask us what we're doing,' but the people want to know, 'Is anyone going to rattle the locks on my place of business after dark?' Well, the answer is that we will. (Intelligarde manager)

According to McLeod, the police were 'distant technocrats' and were incapable of addressing client needs. In the vacuous chasm left in their wake, Intelligarde was offering to step in with the support of prevailing political winds and discontented consumers:

Do you know what's happening in the U.S.? They're using cardboard cut-outs of cruisers to slow traffic in highways. Some merchants are actually pooling their money and buying old cruisers, repainting and washing them daily, just so it appears that the police are around. People are starved for the type of service we can provide for them. (Intelligarde manager)

In the digitally prefigured city of the Law Enforcement Company, these scenes of desperation would be eliminated because everyone would be able to purchase an electronic checkpoint, and someone in a uniform would be there to strike it. And the process of surveillance would be open to all without mystification.

The capacity to monitor security officers and make them accountable and known can also be applied to other populations. The surveillance system can be widened so that workers in disparate locales can also be policed. Here, the nature of private policing is further revealed: it is a surveillance system that is inherently a management system for hire. Plans are being formulated to detach Intelligarde's communications centre and resell it as an international monitoring business. The digital assemblages of the parapolice surveillance system could be transplanted to the most remote reaches of Canada and the world. The new system being imagined would be able to receive over 600 check-ins per hour for service staff across the country. Each client would be able to leave recordings for its staff as well as news and other instructions. The service person would have to check in from a prescribed phone at a designated location.

This applies to home care professionals as well. They have to call in from a predetermined phone, which will automatically be set in the computer. If someone is not calling from where they're supposed to, we'll know. (Intelligarde manager)

Not surprisingly, Intelligarde's managers are considering assigning electronic checkpoint wands or guns to track the movements of workers in isolated locations or in conditions of limited or no supervision. The employees would have to hit stations throughout the facility and download this information into a console; this information would immediately be relayed for analysis to a computer at Intelligarde headquarters. Any anomalies would alert the hyperpanoptic registry; clients (or in this case absentee managers) would then be notified.

The Law Enforcement Company is a contracted policing service in the full and historic sense of that term. Its mandate is to maintain order by knowing the places, spaces, and movements of the people it is charged with monitoring. The company charges itself with both crime control and the hyperpanoptic surveillance of those it is entrusted with monitoring – including its own security officers. By managing a disciplinary regime across its own employees, Intelligarde can successfully flog its risk-reducing ability within a politicized and fear-inducing neoliberal risk market. It endlessly knows its own private police, just as its private police endlessly know others. In practice, the parapolice become the contracted inspectorate for a plurality of state and corporate organizations seeking to purchase both the transparent labour (Lyon, 1994: 119–30) of security work and its techniques for producing transparency in others.

In this chapter I have not considered the multiple modes of resistance employed by both the parapolice and the subject populations they are tasked with controlling; my intention, rather, has been to entertain the complete managerial fantasy of control. I hope I have revealed the risk-reducing, actuarial practices and their correlative modes of surveillance and discipline. The properties of social control endemic to policing institutions in late modernity revolve around the collection of information and the proliferation of that information as a means of commodifying security. The apparatuses of surveillance, which are characteristic of risk society, signal their commodified nature through the virtual panoptics of the Deister system, GPD systems, and centralized communication. The saleability of these security accoutrements demonstrates both the mode of production and the mode of information in which they are fabricated. In other words, the system must produce knowledge about the populations meant to be policed *and* those doing the policing so that the disciplinary techniques of the company will be attractive to the consumer. Thus, the security product being sold reflects an integrated risk management system. In the next chapter I examine how this management model can be little more than 'fantasy,' once the lived realities of those imagined within the assemblage are revealed.

SIX

Solidarity, Fear, and Subculture

Police subculture is a well-documented social phenomenon. The early works of Skolnick (1966), Westley (1970), and others (e.g., Manning and Van Maanen, 1978) demystified the working environments and occupational mores of the men who make up the 'thin blue line.' More recent investigations have continued to focus on the attributes of police work (e.g., Chan, 1996; Ericson and Shearing, 1986; Manning, 1996, 1997; Rigakos, 1995), for the purpose of understanding the effects of 'recipe rules,' 'dramas of control,' and experiential constructions on official (and unofficial) police mobilizations. So much qualitative information has been amassed about the occupational culture of policing that Johnston (1992:186) has criticized 'sociology's preoccupation with front-line police behaviour.' He argues that attention needs to be diverted to the top of the policing pyramid, lest theorists be endlessly embroiled in the microsociological minutiae of street-level practices.

Of course, analyses of the imaginaries of surveillance power and analyses of the forms of resistance and negotiation that constitute dialectics of control are equally valuable to sociological theorizing. In the previous chapter I described how Intelligarde's perpetual system of examination and its hyperpanoptic imagination virtualizes and digitizes the environments to be policed, the employees who police it, and those falling within its gaze. In this chapter I am concerned with describing how both security officers and suspects resist the apparatuses of control constructed by the Law Enforcement Company. I also wish to explore the embattled yet resilient body of parapolice officers, with their constituent 'wannabe' and pugilistic elements. The bravado and the caution of Intelligarde security officers stem from conditions of dependent uncertainty and status frustration and from the fear of being swarmed by angry mobs. This constant risk taking and/or risk aversion results in a strong occupational ethic of interdependence in the face of immediate or impending dangers. This is not unlike the occupational codes of public police agencies, whose numbers tend to heavily emphasize organizational and occupational mobilization in response to threats or violence against their members.

But the parapolice culture is qualitatively different from that of the public police because of what I will later describe as its romanticized 'legionnaire' characteristics. Security officers rely heavily on their fellow officers, and in doing so internalize subcultural norms relating to emergency response and risky incidents. This results in frustration, isolation, and unceasing emotional anxiety. The collective psyche of the parapolice that has developed from this produces contradictory and skewed responses ranging from resigned martyrdom to perpetual dread to fierce fraternal allegiance. These mores act on a security officer in various ways in the course of a single shift, rotation, month, year, or career.

Resistance from Within: The Art of 'Ghosting'

The Intelligarde surveillance system is far from perfect. Despite a hyper-panoptic gaze of continuous digital examination, security officers have found plenty of room to manoeuvre within the virtual system. Intelligarde's Deister system demands constant reporting through the swiping of either coded checkpoints or occurrence strips; yet these closed-ended and automating duties can actually free up security officers for 'non-revenue' actions. Bogard considers the ability to evade or fool electronic detection (1996: 100–13) when he builds on the thoughts of de Certeau (1986) on *la perruque*, 'the wig.' It has been realized for years that 'looking busy,' 'looking productive,' and 'going through the motions' are endemic to police work (Skolnick, 1966; see also Smith and Gray, 1983). At the same time, these things are far harder to do under a system of perpetual examination.

La perruque is about reclaiming personal time from the monotony of work. It is about fooling supervision, surveillance, or – in the case of Intelligarde – the Deister system, the intention of which is to make security officers constantly known to management. It is appropriate, I think, that Intelligarde security officers have called this practice 'ghosting.' By this term, Intelligarde employees have adeptly captured the quality of their presence within the matrix of checkpoints and closed-ended occurrences they must virtually inhabit. The act of being seen is merely a simulation of the *real* disordered and chaotic streets and buildings they actually traverse. Their existence within the virtual and wired city of (Intelligarde's) Toronto is spectral in nature, fleeting and indeterminate, and only a representational strategy:

> Workers find ways to utilize their work*time* to resist the *spatial* control strategies of their employers or, more simply put, to elude workplace surveillance and discipline. These temporal manoeuvres, which take advantage of contingencies within the architectural and political order of the workplace, take place 'out of view,' unnoticed by supervisors (or their optical-mechanical surrogates, cameras, listening devices, monitors). (Bogard, 1996, emphasis in original)

Ghosting is about seeming to be somewhere doing something necessary to the production of surveillance when, in fact, time is being diverted to one's personal use or leisure. Many security officers were reluctant to discuss ghosting on tape but did comment when the recorder was turned off. But I also observed many times how ghosting is accomplished in the satellite workplaces of the Law Enforcement Company. The most obvious method of ghosting is completing 'hits' (or site visits) ahead of the allocated time reserved for such patrols. A security officer can often complete the swiping of Deister checkpoints for a small building within two or three minutes, while the patrols might be scheduled for twenty. Security officers are instructed to stay on sight after the last checkpoint has been struck but of course they do not always do so. A common tactic is to strike half the Deister checkpoints at a building, and then drive away to visit a nearby static site officer, or to rendezvous with another mobile security officer. Often, mobile officers take deliveries of coffee or food to static site officers, or generally socialize with other security officers before returning to the site after fifteen minutes to strike the remaining Deister strips. To all intents and purposes, the Deister collector report will show that the security officer was on site for the required time. Some more daring mobile security officers will actually strike all of the Deister checkpoints and then sign off from the site many kilometres away, since the 'on site' and 'off site' Deister strips are generic ones carried by all security officers in their portfolios.

Most security officers are careful not to report when they arrive and leave a site to the dispatchers, so that they can negotiate their patrol time. This allows for greater 'down time' and opportunity for leisure activities. Mobile officers often radio communications officers with a long list of 'on' and 'off' site times. Although this is not permitted, communications officers typically ignore this procedural dictum because of their close social connections to veteran mobile security officers, or because mobile officers typically take deliveries of take-out food to the dispatchers. In this sense, *la perruque* is a collective effort borne out of a process of reciprocity between workers.

Another variation of 'the wig' involves inflating incidents in order to free up more time for resting or for avoiding work. While on patrol, a security officer may come across a trespasser who, without incident, leaves the property. The mobile officer can then use the occurrence to eat into his patrol time, so that a number of Deister checkpoints can be 'justifiably' missed. Although the incident and paperwork may have taken a few minutes, a tired security officer could stretch it into many more. In this regard, occurrences can also be feigned. These feigned violations will be minor ones that do not require additional paperwork other than mention on the patrol report. A simple swipe of the related occurrence Deister strip allows the security officer to bypass the full patrol.

In the parapolice subculture, there is unbridled disdain for the Deister system and for security officers who overproduce by striking hundreds of checkpoints per shift:

You see these fucking guys hitting a hundred, two hundred Deisters. What the fuck are they doing? It's like a fucking Easter egg hunt. Is that police work? You miss so much when you do that. It's like they're stepping over sleepers and loiterers to hit the fucking thing. 'Oh, excuse me sir, I just have to get that Deister. Can you move your crack can?' (mobile security officer – male)

Producing surveillance may be a sign of successful security work for Intelligarde management, but in the parapolice subculture it is a symptom of poor police work:

What does it prove if I hit a lot of Deisters? Does it mean I'm a good officer? You know, it's something they want and some guys are out there running around like chickens with their heads cut off but that doesn't prove anything to me. (mobile security officer – male)

Regression toward the mean in security work is promoted by a subculture intent on teaching 'cherries' that hitting Deister strips does not endear them to their colleagues. On the other hand, security officers who are interested in promotion or recognition may produce far higher Deister counts than their fellow officers. One officer led all others in average Deister hits while he was preparing for the PRO competition. For their part, management posts Deister production numbers to 'close the gap' (Foucault, 1977) between the body of security officers. High producers are rewarded with praise; low Deister counts reflect badly on the entire platoon. This is intended to increase peer pressure on security officers who are not vigilant in this regard.

Another mode of surveillance and accountability is the Intelligarde Clear Net radio system, which according to the description I offered in the previous chapter should promote isolationism, general anomie, and centralized decision-making. If all communication was filtered through communications headquarters, as was intended, then this would work quite nicely. Of course, in practice it does not. Many security officers refuse to keep their radios keyed to the communications centre; instead they prefer to communicate with a nearby partner, site security officer, or mobile district officer. The radio system pre-empts general radio traffic over an open frequency, but does allow for unchecked communication between security officers on innumerable private channels. This results in an unofficial chain of communication between security officers negotiating a wide variety of unsanctioned mobilizations.

Instead of relying on communications officers to orchestrate back-up and support, many security officers call district colleagues ahead of an actual incident or occurrence. According to most parapolice officers, one of the most troubling aspects of the Mike system is the lack of an open frequency, which stunts a collective sense of imminent danger and thus impedes preventive actions. For example, in the past, when a security officer was about to make an arrest and thought he might be outnumbered, a neighbouring security officer could overhear and volunteer support. Since many mobile officers withhold information about their current whereabouts from dispatch, communications officers must call out to a series of security officers in order to ascertain their proximity and ability to assist. In the eyes of many officers, this highly centralized system is inefficient and dangerous. Thus, unofficial communications take place – parapolice officers call ahead and check support and back-up on their own. These mobilizations are accomplished without information being forwarded to the communications office.

While a 'group call' function is available to the security officers, they believe it is too expensive to be used except in emergencies. One officer told me that 'it costs over 400 dollars to activate a group call'; another security officer estimated the cost in the thousands of dollars. Yet another mobile security officer noted that 'group calls are a last resort – even [the president] hears the message on his personal radio at home.' This security officer chooses to negotiate his own support in lieu of official company mobilizations, because he does not want to be held accountable for its misuse. For many security officers, it is even scarier that only one line to the dispatchers can be activated at once. This means that they may very well get a busy signal when calling for help. This last problem is anathema to the occupational code of Intelligarde International, since at its core is an ethic of mutual assistance. The company's attempts to structure and centralize the flow of information have resulted in a wholesale rejection of the radio system and the building of a network of unofficial information exchanges and mobilizations that are never documented on official report forms or broadcast to the communications centre. I recorded at least fifteen such incidents.

On one occasion a mobile security officer hurrying to assist a fellow officer lit his vehicle's police light bars to help clear the traffic ahead. He sped dangerously through downtown traffic, shouting 'You're not seeing this!' This incident was never reported to dispatch, and had we been stopped by the public police, charges could have been laid under the Highway Traffic Act for speeding and for using emergency lights on public roadways.

The Mike system has facilitated socializing by Intelligarde officers, in that closed frequencies allow for sustained and insulated discussions. Inadvertently, the radio system has spawned an expansive informal communication system hidden to management.

The favourite pastime of Intelligarde security officers is socializing, trading gossip, and exchanging information on police recruiting in informal gatherings. I was often used as a rationale for such meetings: when transferring me from district to district, mobile security officers would meet at well-manned static sites for the 'escort exchange.' This often resulted in gatherings of five or more security officers at a given site. There is a strong need in the subculture for such meetings, which reinforce bonds between officers and also produce visible displays of authority, solidarity, and cohesion for tenants and 'bad guys.' This is good for the morale of site security officers, because it reminds loiterers and dealers that support is available to those officers.

'Ghosting' is not a secret term in the parapolice subculture. Intelligarde managers know full well that it goes on – after all, they have also spent time in patrol duties. They are considering adding more all-encompassing surveillance techniques to their repertoire, such as GPDs, a new radio system, and vehicle monitors. In the meantime, current hyperpanoptic apparatuses are buttressed by vigilant supervision. This mostly involves the QCM following, or shadowing, security officers on patrol. If a security officer is not at the same site as he reported to dispatch, the QCM may seize his run sheets and Deister gun to examine his whereabouts.

These activities are unpopular with some security officers, who note that 'sneaking about' is devious and shows mistrust:

D lives, eats, and sleeps Intelligarde. He thinks everybody else should too. That, for me, is not going to happen ... He's been known to sneak up on people on the job, you know. That, for me, is not what a supervisor should be doing. There are two ways to make people work for you: they fear you, or they respect you. This company is run on fear and constant supervision. (mobile security officer – male)

However, most security officers accept that attention from management comes from repeated abuses and that oversight is simply the nature of security work. They respect managerial inspection but fear that it may sometimes be arbitrary:

There have been guys fired from this company, just like that [snaps fingers]. You should ask around. It's unfair, when you think about it. Some guys were knobs and deserve it. My opinion is that most of these guys did deserve it, but what happens if I make a mistake? Am I history? (mobile security officer – male)

I think D does a good job and I respect his position, but sometimes he comes on too strong. Most guys here I think respect him, but he's also rubbed guys the wrong way too so they have a grudge. As far as I'm concerned, I don't fuck the dog so I have nothing to worry about. (static site officer – male)

Many security officers are concerned that a double-standard exists between managerial and line officer accountability – that the intense scrutiny and high standard of performance demanded of the parapolice does not apply for Intelligarde managers:

If there's a problem, then there's a chain of command that has to be followed in order to rectify something. So, if I've got a payroll problem, I have to go through the supervisor, who then sends it to someone else and then it gets to payroll. For them, no one is accountable. For me, I'm always accountable. If I fuck up, I'm history. What happens if management fucks up, which they do regularly? Nothing, it's just a mistake. (mobile security officer – male)

When a manager does make an error, the parapolice subculture quickly diffuses the incident to other line officers. This serves to delegitimize supervisory orders – stories of managerial blunders induce employee indifference to directions. I once observed a chain of secrecy and coded communications by a number of security officers on a given platoon. In the incident they at first kept from me, an Intelligarde supervisor left a handgun, without a trigger lock and outside the lockbox, in the trunk of a company cruiser. This incident was used as a foil for entering into a general discussion of the inadequacies of management. Most security officers went along with the complaints; others later confided to me that their colleagues sometimes 'whine too much.'

Crime Fighting and the Wannabe Culture

The subculture of the Intelligarde parapolice cannot be understood without an examination of the shared experiences and frustrations of its members. Subcultural orientations dictate that these shared, subjective, aversive experiences hone a necessary rationale for deviant behaviour.

Almost all Intelligarde security officers want careers in law enforcement. They are young, energetic, and eager to be hired by public policing agencies. Most would like to join the Metropolitan Toronto Police Service, but others are not particularly selective about where they end up. Some Intelligarde security officers have applied to police departments as far away as New York, Boston, Houston, and New Orleans. This 'wannabe' subculture instils a sense of collective purpose among security officers. Everyone wants law enforcement experience, and everyone is undergoing recruit screening or has information about police departments that are hiring. This continuous exchange of information about physical and psychological tests and personal interviews provides a common social grounding and important preparatory information. Many officers from the Law Enforcement Company have moved into careers in public policing. This is heartening for those officers still with Intelligarde. Placements to public police agencies buttress the organization's commitment to professional law enforcement and send a message to security officers that their efforts are supported. Intelligarde managers do not hesitate to reschedule shifts and provide off days for employees who must undergo police testing during one of their rotations.

It is not surprising, then, that Intelligarde security officers measure their success against law enforcement ideals – 'good pinches,' court testimony, and crime control:

I was trying to arrest a guy in a stairwell for smoking crack and we got into an altercation and he wouldn't leave so I tried to place him under arrest for failing to leave when directed ... He just went offside and we were in a stairwell so I couldn't call to anyone ... We ended up fighting in the stairwell for a good five or six minutes. And he was huge, probably twice as big as me. And he was throwing me around the stairwell like a dart. I had back-up coming but they just weren't getting there quick enough, you know ... I had this guy pinned three times and every time he broke free and I thought, 'Man, this is it,' because I just couldn't handle this guy ... He took off down Pembroke Street and one of our guys off duty had his radio and spotted him on Shuter and radioed his position to everyone else. He couldn't get him because he wasn't in uniform. But he pointed him out to our guys as two of our cruisers closed in. The guy was hunched over and out of breath. We grabbed him and he still had fifty dollars worth of crack on him. Metro showed up and got the arrest. I just had court for that three weeks ago ... He eventually got six months and two years' probation. (mobile security officer – male)

Most Intelligarde officers can relate a story about a 'good pinch' while at the company. One officer investigated and arrested a suspect on Intelligarde property at the request of an MTP sergeant. In this case, the security officer was being deployed in lieu of public police response:

I guess my best pinch was one time I was shooting the shit with this Metro sergeant and he gets a call over the radio that there's a suspicious person in behind one of our lots on Bleeker Street. So the guy, he's from 51 Division, asks me to check it out since it was on one of our sites. I go around back and find the guy who fit the description – blue blazer, baseball cap. So I arrest him and find a spark plug he was using to smash the car windows with in his hand. Anyways, the guy was charged with three counts of possession of stolen property and other stuff. I've got court for that one next week. That was a nice, clean, easy one. (mobile/static officer – male)

Dangerous arrests that are handled without the assistance of the local public police are considered especially meritorious. In the following incident, the security officer and his partner may have saved a woman from rape and possible murder:

My partner and I got called to an apartment where there was a guy living in there who we had ongoing problems with. The neighbour had called and said that he heard a female inside the next-door apartment screaming for help and he thought there was some kind of domestic going on. So we got there and we know this guy. I mean he's a crack head, he's a problem child, he's done all sorts of crime. So anyways, when we got there, we bang on the door and we can hear the female inside calling, 'Help!' 'Help me!' You know? 'Let me go!' 'He's grabbing me!' And all sorts of things. So we banged on the door and announced who we were and he told us to get lost and started screaming at us to mind our own business and that it had nothing to do with us. But we could hear inside that tables and chairs were being thrashed around and someone was in need of help. So two seconds before we were about to kick in the door, he opens the door and a female comes running out with her face covered in blood and her pants all ripped and goes tearing off down the hallway. 'He's trying to rape me!' You know? 'He's trying to rape me!' And he comes out all foaming at the mouth, all hyped up on crack or whatever, and he's armed himself with a billiard stick, a pool stick. So we tried talking to him and de-escalating, but nothing was working. He was just intent on fighting with us. Sure enough, the pool stick came up, and he was about to hit us with it, so we got into it with him, and we were restraining him, and I was trying to get the stick out of his hand. I knew that if he got his hand free, someone was going to get clobbered with it. I couldn't break his grip – he was pretty strong and he was pretty high – so I ended up having to hit him across the knuckles here with my mag-lite. And I got told later on that I apparently broke two of his knuckles ... I actually got court for that next week. He got forcible confinement, sexual assault, assault with a deadly weapon, and all kinds of stuff. (mobile security officer – Male)

I asked the security officer why the tenant hadn't called the police. 'Because we *are* the police in that area,' he replied, 'and by the time they come the woman would be dead.' As far as the security officer was concerned, the woman would have been looking at a two to three hour wait unless it was a 911 emergency call. 'Besides,' the officer added, 'we're just as capable of handling it as Metro.'

The best remembered and most often retold stories related to arrests made before or despite the involvement of the public police. In the following incident, officers of the Law Enforcement Company captured a wanted person before the police could on an Intelligarde property. This arrest was considered a success for the entire firm because it involved two sites and demonstrated the organization's communication capabilities and its officers' vigilance:

One of our best pinches, I think, was when this one lady stabbed a guy on one of our properties and fled. Metro was looking for her, and the call went out, but we also had a description because we knew what was going on. Three hours later we arrested her on another one of our properties for attempted murder and turned her over to Metro. Because, as I'm sure you know by now, we control a major section of the downtown core from Bloor and Sherbourne to St Hubert and the Esplanade – that's ours. So she was making her way through our adjoining sites. (mobile security officer – male)

The zeal of Intelligarde officers to make arrests sometimes leads them onto shaky legal ground. On one occasion, Intelligarde officers pursued a suspect in what amounted to a car chase through the city. The suspect finally jumped from his vehicle while it was in gear. Had the incident not ended so fortunately, Intelligarde could have faced legal repercussions:

About a year and a half ago. We had a guy working Parking Authority of Toronto and he caught a guy prying a cash drawer from one of the booths. He got to his car and took off. So our guy got into his car and took off after him. It was kinda cool. They were headed west through the city. I was headed east through the city and we just sort of kept on going till we were gonna meet up not really knowing where till we finally got together. Dispatch was on the phone to Metro giving them directions as we were calling them out. The guy bailed out of his car, left it in gear, and took off down the street. We chased him down, took him to the ground, 'cuffed him. And there was a whole pile of people watching. We got him down, kept him down, kept him in 'cuffs until the cops showed up ... that was a nice one. I think the cops were a little jealous. But they were really good, they were patting us on the back, telling us we did a good job. The sergeant showed up and was yelling, 'You shouldn't have been doing that,' and then on the side was kinda like saying, 'That was a pretty good arrest on that.' (static site officer – male)

Some Intelligarde stories, like the following one, border on the incredible. The more notable Intelligarde interventions reflect 'real police work':

There's stories up at the Kipling building. Two of our guys found a carload full of machine guns, Uzis, and a shotgun. Have you heard this one with the machine guns? This one is phenomenal, ... oh my God, you haven't heard it? They picked up the guns and say, 'Whoa, we have to call the cops' ... in the underground. Well, the guys who own the cars are coming around the corner –

'What are you guys doing with our cars?' [Our guys] ended up getting shot at and so one of our guys that was holding an Uzi started shooting back at them. So, this is the type of stuff ... This was before the second last time we lost it [the site]. We always lose that site. We're our own worst enemy because we clean it up and they hire some crappy security company and we're back where we started again. We've had and lost that site so many times that we just leave it on the listing now. (mobile security officer – male)

I have already indicated by statistical data that the parapolice are involved in crime control. Thirty-eight per cent of Intelligarde incidents involve the public police (see Table 3.5). Past research in Canada indicates that police officers view security guards as 'Mickey Mouse' in training, deportment, and mandate. This is especially evident in their understandings and constructions of the private security sector's loss prevention focus (Shearing, Stenning, and Addario, 1985b). Considering that, and considering the zeal and bravado with which Intelligarde officers sometimes carry out their crime control duties, and considering that Intelligarde and the MTP are in regular contact, it is little wonder that the former sometimes come into conflict with the latter:

There was this one guy who was loaded, and I tried to arrest him because he was pissing on the property. So I go to arrest him, and I apply a very simple procedure on him, but he's flinging at me, and when I take him down the guy is bleeding all over the place because he banged his head while going down. The cops arrive and ask me what happened. And when I told them they're like, 'What, you did this to the guy because he was peeing?' And of course, now they think I went to town on this guy and all that happened was that he landed on his head. They said that he could actually charge me for assault if I charged him. So I said, just get this guy out of here on the trespass. So they ended up letting him go because they thought he already suffered enough. (mobile security officer – male)

Sometimes, however, Intelligarde officers serve almost as auxilliaries of the public police:

I don't know if anybody has already told you this, but everybody calls me the traffic cop. I work out in the west end where there's a lot of highways. I'm out there every night, and I've done a lot of impaireds. In the last two years ... I follow them on the road, and I radio the cops, and it's very crucial that, you know, it's not like I'm an ordinary citizen. You have to know what they're looking for:

weaving, changing lanes, acceleration, deceleration, erratic driving. They'll ask, 'What did you observe?' In the last four months, I've done about six. I have a lot of downtime. The last one, I called OPP. I don't want to tie up dispatch with non-revenue items. (mobile security officer – male)

Clearly, Intelligarde officers' relations with the public police often reflect specific histories with the various services or divisions. Where the police and Intelligarde have consistently got along well, personal ties may develop between public officers and the parapolice. These can evolve into student–mentor relationships:

I get along with them. No problems. The only time they get upset with our guys is when we go beyond our job. (mobile security officer)

Metro many times will instil this teacher–student relationship by looking for what you did wrong. They'll point out where you went wrong in the arrest. They won't dwell on it, but they'll let you know where you basically fucked up. (mobile security officer – male)

Well, I guess because I've been here for so long, they coach us. They tell us how to do things and get around stuff. They say, 'If you can't handle it, give us a call.' They help us with how the law works. (static site officer – male)

As far as dispatch, we have to deal with Metro dispatch daily, if not hourly. So there's a mutual respect. As far as the cops down here, I find that I get rides in from the bridge and stuff. They're good guys. But I guess in some other areas that isn't necessarily the case. I hear stories from the guys coming on or off shift and it's sad to learn that some cops don't give a shit, you know. But others are great. A lot of it has to do with youth, I think. (communications officer – male)

In other locales, relations between the public and the private police depend on the individuals involved. Transactions range from the amicable to the adversarial:

It varies. It depends on the officer. It's the same as if I was Joe Citizen. Everyone has had good and bad experiences with the police. I swear to you that some police officers turn around and follow us and if I go one kilometre over the speed limit they'll pull me over. They go out of their way to follow the cars and some will just casually wave. They'll turn around and follow you right up your ass, and if you've got an alarm response, you're screwed. (mobile security officer – male)

23 Division has been really cooperative with us. Whenever we've had arrests, they've responded very quickly. All of our arrests, the majority have been issued POTs, provincial offences tickets. (static site officer – male)

It depends on where you're working. Each division has its own positive or negative views of Intelligarde. For example, 23 Division had a very negative view of Intelligarde because we had some real just bad instances where security officers overexceeded their authority or did bad arrests. That sort of thing. And it took a lot of work with a steady crew in that area to set up a good working relationship ... because they had a real sour taste in their mouths after working with some of our officers. (communications officer – male)

According to many Intelligarde officers, they get along but with the public police in downtown Toronto, where the various divisions are accustomed to their presence. Some outlying divisions and police services do not have the same professional relationship with the Law Enforcement Company:

We work well with the Metro police generally in the downtown area. When you get out to some of the outskirt areas, they tend not to be very useful to us. One of the divisions, I needed back-up once. They came, drove around the parking lot, didn't see anybody and left. (mobile security officer – male)

It varies from division to division. The guys downtown we get along with. There's, I think, a mutual respect there. We do our jobs and stay out of their way. Out in the suburbs, especially out in the west end, I think a lot of police, the public police, see us as their rivals ... like we're trying to be them or trying to do their job ... But of course, we're trying to do a job similar to that on an entirely different level with an entirely different set of rules. (mobile security officer – male)

It depends on their past experiences with us. I was working out in 23 Division, and I heard that the cops were assholes and this and that. But I did what I had to do. I had the paperwork for them when they got there, and by the end I was playing hockey with them on Thursday nights. Cops know when they come out here, they're going to have everything they need. All they have to do is write the ticket or take the guy in. (static site officer – male)

Intelligarde officers report that the public may or may not respect them. It depends on the population they are policing, the population they are policing *for*, and the general environment of policing:

You get some people who will treat you like a police officer. You'll get some people who will treat you like you're nothing. Out here, in Peel, they're a higher class of people. But they're basically helpless snobs that don't have a clue. They'll call and say, 'Come quick, the kids are making noise,' and if you're a couple of minutes over your expected time they'll start beaking at you. They're real idiots. It's hard to respect their pettiness after coming from St James Town and North York, you know? (mobile security officer – male)

The negative view that a lot of people have about us gets a little frustrating. You're there and you're trying to help people and you're dealing with a bunch of people that don't want you to help them. They see you as making an imposition on their lifestyle or something and it gets very frustrating. (mobile security officer – male)

The store community, they really support us. They [others] criticize us because they think we're arresting someone because they're black. I have to watch for the crowd because they'll come and try to help him. If I think that it's going to be a bad arrest or that there are too many people in the area ... If you call for back-up you're gonna get a riot. You're going to get a lot of people who are going to help this one person who maybe stole something from K-Mart. And then you've got guards fighting or holding people back. So, the best thing to do sometimes is just to let it go ... In the three years I've been here, we've had about five severe swarmings. (static site officer – male)

These comments are in line with previous research on public perceptions of private security. Shearing and colleagues (1985c: 227) note that 'private security has not established itself as a stereotypic cultural object about which people have clear and distinct images.' It is also true, however, that Intelligarde carries a reputation of swift and severe action against the populations it is charged with policing. This is illustrated by a security officer who argues that he benefits from Intelligarde's 'no nonsense' reputation:

I don't know if they respect us as much as fear us. Intelligarde has the reputation where you don't screw with us. Or if you do, you'll have six cruisers there in about five minutes. And like look at me, I'm not the most intimidating guy. I'm not six feet, 200 pounds. I like when I'm doing my patrol that I can hear guys saying don't screw with Intelligarde because you're going to have six guys here in five minutes. So that works for me when I do my patrols, because it's not like, 'Oh, he's just some numbkey [?] security guard.' (mobile security officer – male)

Despite all of the bravado, Intelligarde officers are a weary lot who feel they get little respect from either the public or the police. This became clear to me one day when a mobile officer I was with responded to a call for a back-up. When we arrived at the site – a downtown rooming house – we saw two black, middle-aged men outside the residence, yelling at a beleaguered security officer. Soon after we arrived, another vehicle and two foot patrol officers joined us from a nearby site. The incident had started when the security officer began making inquiries about the occupants of the house. One of the individuals should not have been there because of a previous banning.

The suspect fled when more officers arrived. While we stood around the front of the house, the resident who had invited the banned individual inside, and had then challenged security, became conciliatory. 'Thanks, man, we cool, right, we cool?' he asked. The officer learned that the resident had not wanted the man there either but had put up a display so as not to look like he was betraying his 'friend.' The man shook the security officer's hand and thanked him.

S/O 1:   [To me] See the type of shit we have to put up with? That guy wanted him out too, but was giving me a hard time. He was belligerent and wouldn't provide a name.

As we turned to leave, an older man staggered toward us as he passed the front of the house. He began to yell over the top of the fence.

Man: Hey, why don't you go home, you fucking wannabes?
S/O 2:   Sir, don't you have anything better to do?
Man: You guys are all just a bunch of fucking wannabes!
S/O 1:   Hey, you're drunk, just go home.
Man: I may be drunk, but at least I'm not a fucking wannabe.
S/O 2:   [To me] This happens every fucking night.
Man: W-a-n-n-a-b-e!!
S/O 1:   Why don't you come here and say that?
Man: Why, so you can arrest me? I may be drunk but I ain't stupid. I'm on public property, you fucking wannabe. You come here. If you so much as touch me I can sue your ass.
S/O 1:   Just come here.
Me: Sir, just go home.
S/O 2:   OK, guys, just forget it.
Man: Fucking wannabes!

S/O 2:   Yeah, we're wannabes. We want to be something, do something. What about you? What are you gonna fucking do, you old drunk? You wan' another drink? Huh, asshole? What do you wannabe? A fucking alcoholic? Now fuck off, old man, we're trying to do our jobs!

The man staggers away, but not before yelling out a few more parting remarks. The status frustration the parapolice experience in performing their duties was aptly summed up by one officer:

Our major obstacle when dealing with the public is the 'security guard' patch. (mobile security officer – male)

Resistance from Below: Safety in Numbers

Private police have always been collectively resisted by the populations they are charged with governing. In early eighteenth-century England,[1] debtors' sanctuaries such as 'the Mint' outside London facilitated routinized criminal activity and resistance to 'lawful' intrusions (McMullan, 1996: 121). These protectorates were havens for thieves, burglars, and prostitutes. Any officials who ventured into this area did so at their own peril (Brewer, 1980). They ran the risk of being thrown into tubs of urine, and tossed into the open sewers that lined the city streets. In 1705 it took four justices of the peace with twenty-one constables battling numerous 'shelterers' to apprehend a bankrupt and his wares. A parapolice officer 292 years later related the following:

Y: This one guy kept saying that he's here to visit his aunt, but he was already banned. So me and my partner tell him to go up and see her but that he can't hang out in the lobby. So he's giving us lip and stuff, and we tell him to leave, and he refuses to do so. So I arrest him for failure to leave ... We attempted to put him in restraints, and he began to struggle with us, so we took him to the ground and tried again, and he kept on struggling. Then we look up and see six guys coming at us.

Me: Where did they come from?

Y: Outside mostly. So we try to get him in restraints and can only get one arm, so we handcuff him to the doorknob in the lobby there. So, within a matter of seconds there was twelve guys on us, and by now we're shitting our pants.

Me: Twelve?

Y: Well, actually by the time we had him up against the wall and cuffed
         to the doorknob there were about thirty-six of them. It's like a pack
         of hyenas. One person would come in, throw a punch and then duck
         out. And then another one would come in ...

Me: How long did it take for help to arrive?

Y: The response time from our company was approximately three min-
         utes until back-up got here. From the moment when we notified
         them that we'd be placing someone under arrest, we knew we had
         back-up coming. And then we radioed that he was resisting arrest
         and then eventually it was 10–33 [emergency], so we had two guys
         running from another site down the street. We also had District 11
         come from the west end.

Me: So I guess you made a group call on the Mike system?

Y: Group call, yes. So then there were about four or five districts here
         and then all of a sudden Metro rolled up. It took about twenty min-
         utes for 23 Division to show up, because for some reason – I don't
         know why – I guess they had another call. So then we handed him
         over to MTP and then we did up statements for them. And then we
         had to go to the hospital, because, myself, I suffered a concussion
         throughout the whole ordeal. I got my head slammed off the floor
         and the pillar when they were on top of us. So I didn't know what
         was going on, so we went to the hospital and my other partner suf-
         fered a broken hand, strained back, and almost a blown out knee ...
         We've had a couple of other smaller swarmings but nothing as big as
         that.

Me: Was 23 Division cooperative when they finally showed up?

Y: Very cooperative.

Me: What did they say about the guy being handcuffed to the doorknob?

Y: Well, they understood that under the situation, that was the best
         thing we could have done. He was under arrest. Once you arrest
         someone you can't let him flee. Because we're not proper authori-
         ties to let him go, we can't issue a POT ... They said we did a good
         job keeping him there because there were guys trying to kick the
         doorknob off. They actually rolled in a couple of units, which helped
         disperse the crowd.

Me: How did all of these people descend on you?

Y: Most of the people we deal with live on the second floor or some of
         the lower floors so they can sell their drugs and they can get down
         the stairs very quickly. The lobby has a camera with monitors in

> everyone's apartments so they can see who's buzzing in, so that's
> how they knew.

Me: So they saw it on their CCTV monitors and ran down.

Y: Yep.

Me: So the CCTV in that case worked against you guys.

Y: Yep. That's right. And it was designed to get the community involved
in their own safety. It didn't work out that way. [*Laughter*]

This attack demonstrates how technologies of surveillance can be turned
against the watcher. Instead of utilizing the CCTV system to assist the
officers or to call the police, the 'community' of dealers employed the
surveillance system as an opportunity to resist the parapolice.

The possibility of racially motivated swarmings is an ever-present
deterrent to parapolicing overzealousness:

If you take down one guy, the way that we work is that you take him down fast
and then get out of the public sight fast. Because otherwise you'll have about
fifty guys on you. (static site officer – male)

The gang-style 'rumbles' that sometimes ensue when Intelligarde security officers attempt arrests on black suspects put black security officers
in an interesting position, yet they maintain that their decisions are not
tainted by skin colour. One black officer noted:

Well, you see, the thing about me is that when I'm doing my work I don't see
colour. I try to blind my eyes to colours. I don't deal with colours when I'm
doing my work. You're black, white, or whatever, if you are doing something
that's wrong I'm gonna give you the full length as I'm trained to do ... They
scorn me just like they scorn anyone around this place because they think we're
all the same pack. You have the average black guy who might say 'hi' to me and
not say 'hi' to B [a white security officer], right? That doesn't mean that they're
gonna be looked at different if they do something wrong because I'm going to
kick their ass just the same. (static site officer – male)

Another black officer has strong feelings about the role of the Law
Enforcement Company in predominantly black neighbourhoods. He
argues that while young residents put up a front of resistance, they are
actually happy the parapolice are there:

I can tell you that this not a racist company. I'm sure that there have been a couple of idiots in the past that are no longer with us who have said things they shouldn't. But I go to sites and I talk to young guys. Kids that act tough around their friends because they live there. I understand that. They say to me, you know, 'I'm glad you guys are here.' Because they know if we were gone, black or white, there would be no order. Nobody wants to live like that. (mobile security officer – male)

In one North York mall, a near-riot broke out when security officers tried to arrest a black suspect:

We got swarmed up here once. One of our guys lost his billy stick and was getting hit in the side of the head with it. Just chaos. And it was free swinging. There were about ten of us here that showed up. When it was all over, we just sat by the water fountain trying to catch our breath. We pointed out all of the guys who were still in restraints or who the police cornered. It was like, 'He assaulted him, that guy assaulted me, that guy tried to choke me,' and on and on. (static site officer – male)

The Intelligarde uniform is unwelcome in many parts of central and north Toronto. Parapolice officers face the very real possibility of violence. The fear of being swarmed is palpable in lobbies and malls governed by the Law Enforcement Company.

'TIPs'[2] and 'Swarmings': The Dialectics of Fear

Private policing has always been a dangerous business. Eighteenth-century descriptions of the self-proclaimed and charismatic 'thief-taker general,' Jonathan Wild, reveal a strong, stocky man who was deeply scarred by his dealings with London's criminal class:

By 1725 he had two fractures in his skull and his bald head was covered with silver plates. He had seventeen wounds in various parts of his body from swords, daggers, and gun-shots, contracted in the innumerable affrays, set-to's and riots he always seemed to be engaged in. His throat had been cut. (Howson, 1970: 245–6)

The threat of imminent danger is an inescapable part of parapolicing in Toronto. In Chapter 3, I noted that Intelligarde security officers are five times more likely than their public police counterparts to be assaulted while on duty. Despite the low probability overall (i.e., only a .748 per cent chance per response – see Table 3.1), stories of 'swarmings' run deep into the subcultural fabric of Intelligarde International.

One specific incident was referred to repeatedly by many officers while I was collecting data in the field. This illustrates the immeasurable impact of subcultural narratives on the general parapolice workforce. I finally met the security officer involved in the swarming, and he told me about the attack.

J:	I guess the things that frighten me are ... I guess multiple persons. When you're confronting multiple persons and you're a solo officer with maybe a canine. I'll give you a little story, just very quickly. About a year ago, just over a year ago, I was working static at a place we do at Jane and Woolner. It's a place we call The Corridor. We got a call – myself and my partner. It's a really, really bad area.
Me:	Yeah.
J:	Anyways, we get a call that there's some guy dealing crack behind one of the buildings. We take a stroll back there and we see one guy so we go up and we start talking to him. Another guy shows up, he's saying to let his buddy go, stop hassling him. We try to keep the two separated ... The second guy that shows up pulls a gun on us. We take him to the ground and within five seconds we were swarmed by about twenty-five guys. We were beaten to a pulp. We linked arms and basically stayed down. I got kicked, punched, I had an X-acto knife stabbed in my neck. I had a champagne bottle smashed over my head and the guy just kept sticking it in my head and literally tore my scalp to shreds.
Me:	Holy ...
J:	The last thing I saw was this guy standing over me taking a two by four to my face ... and then it was lights out. Yeah, and I guess you don't even have time to be scared in a situation like that but that's what everybody fears happening to them.
Me:	And you're still doing it?
J:	I was back a week later. My nose wasn't even busted but I still had black eyes.
Me:	How did you guys deal with that situation?
J:	We went unconscious, basically.
Me:	No, I mean after ...
J:	Afterwards? The manpower up there was stepped up a little bit, and then we essentially went back to doing what we do every day. That's my job. It's one of the grim realities of doing my job. And that was

the second time I was swarmed. I've been swarmed three times so far in this company. That was by far the worst. The other time I was arresting a drunk driver on our property, and I got swarmed by about twenty people who just kicked and punched. There were no weapons involved. I got out of that one relatively unscathed. I had back-up very quickly with canine and they were able to keep the group off while I made the full arrest.

Me: So ...

J: I mean, stuff like that is a grim reality. We could go into a stairwell right now and run into three or four people who are smoking crack or shooting heroine. They're completely unpredictable. They could have an open-capped syringe that's got Hepatitis B or C or HIV on it and if they stick you with that it's over. You're done. Yet you're still required to stop these guys and put them into custody. We don't have the use-of-force options that Metro police have – we have our hands, and we have a flashlight, and we have our mouths.

J's partner took considerably longer to return to duty. The effects of the assault had a more pronounced psychological effect on him. He did eventually return to work and is currently assigned to Toronto's downtown bus terminal.

Gang assaults on Intelligarde security officers are not considered rare, or isolated incidents. They are considered part of the possibility if not the *probability* of patrol work:

I don't like dealing with a large group. That's the biggest fear I've had. That never really hit until I worked at our Kipling and Steeles site, that's where we got swarmed ... This one was in May. We had the site for three days. And we were making an arrest on one person and it ended up with thirty-six of them on top of us. (static site officer – male)

I'm afraid when I'm arresting someone because I don't know how the people are going to react. If it's one person I can handle it. It's the people around him ... I'm like everybody else, nobody wants to be swarmed. We patrol some very political areas and anything can happen. (static site officer – male)

Considering all this, it is hardly surprising that quick response and a more of mutual aid are central to the occupational climate of parapolicing. If one ingredient can be isolated away as the most important in the general subcultural ethic of Intelligarde security officers, it is the code of mutual assistance:

The worst fear is getting jumped and having lax back-up. In Peel, there's no back-up. There's one other officer but he's usually closer to the Etobicoke border. So if I'm out at Winston Churchill, I'm screwed. (mobile security officer – male)

I fear not being able to call for back-up. Sometimes we're on the third level of an underground parking area and if something happens down there I'm all alone with a flashlight and body armour. The radios don't work through five feet of concrete. Some sites actually have repeaters but that's still not enough. If they have weapons and confront me, what am I supposed to do? You can't run. Everybody has that fear. All you have is your radio, your dog if you have one, and your partner. (mobile security officer – male)

One especially eloquent officer summed up the plight of Intelligarde employees by referring to their isolation, constant anxiety, and lack of respect from the police and public. His romanticized construction of the parapolice is telling of the occupational culture he inhabits:

It also gets to your head when you spend twelve hours of your day patrolling underground lots and shitty stairwells across the city. You only see crap and you get crapped on by the dealers, the druggies, the prostitutes, and some of the tenants. You know, you're on patrol and people think you're just a wannabe, or a fucking racist, and it gets to you. The worst thing of all is when on top of all of that, the cops, who should sympathize and understand, they shit on you too after risking your life in some fucking dark alley at two a.m. It's disheartening ... For the money we make, sometimes I think we're the last true, bona fide, and unsung heroes of the city. And the only people that know that are our fellow officers. That's why we can't let each other down. Because no one is gonna help us. The tenants pile on top of you in a swarming, the newspapers think you're 'Intelligoons,' and the cops arrive after half an hour. If I don't rush over there to help an officer, who else is? I know it, he knows it, we all know it. (static site officer – male)

The corollary of not getting support in dangerous situations is not being able to provide it or failing to get to a scene quickly enough. Intelligarde security officers who have been in swarmings remember exactly how long it took for their colleagues and for the police to arrive. No one wants to be the last one to arrive in relief of a fellow officer. And no one wants to fail their friends on their platoon. This is why Intelligarde officers often break the law and activate their vehicle's emergency lights to get through traffic in support of an officer in distress:

I'm afraid all the time, actually. The whole thing is running on adrenaline ... Yeah, I'm absolutely afraid of swarmings, but honestly the thing I'm most afraid of is not knowing where to go when somebody else needs my help. I mean that fucks me up. When they put me out there, you know, they put me in the west end district not knowing of the demographics of the sites, not knowing the type of people there, which they definitely need to do. So that's why in the briefing today I was asking for a new site list, 'cause my old one is shit – it didn't have all of them on there. (mobile security officer – male)

I guess my biggest worry is not being able to get somewhere and help out one of the other officers who needs my help. As a mobile officer, you're the back-up to all static sites in the area. If they get into the real deep shit, my biggest worry is being able to get there in time to help. (mobile security officer – male)

My biggest fear, bar none, is dropping a call ... That means not getting people there quickly enough or not being aware of what's going on. I couldn't live with myself if someone got hurt because I fucked up. (communications officer – male)

Of course, the above fears are only the most powerful. There are others:

The scariest thing lately has been the alarms where you don't know what's going on. Especially motion alarms in secluded areas. You have to check things out before calling Metro. You have to go into backyards bordering ravines or wooded lots in the middle of the night. Who knows what's back there? The other thing, of course, is being outnumbered. Especially if back-up is miles away. But being swarmed, that's high on everyone's list. (mobile security officer – male)

Anyone who's on drugs or alcohol is a problem. That scares me. I can talk my way out of most altercations, but where I am there's hardly any trouble. I'm looking after the cars of affluent people in the Yonge-Eglinton area. You know, constant motorized patrol. So it's not like I'm in any imminent danger. (mobile security officer – female)

Overzealous 'cherries' (new officers – see Chapter 4) who constantly 'cry wolf' after getting themselves involved in dangerous situations are widely resented. Veteran officers have few social ties with new recruits, and generally do not trust them to size up potential hazards:

A lot of times I'm afraid some of these stupid and gung-ho young guys are going to get me killed. They can also fuck up an entire site because they want to kick some ass and they make it dangerous for you in the future. I'm older, but I've got to go when called to a site. They're playing with my health. (mobile security officer – male)

The thing that's the worst is when new guys are trying to make a name for themselves or don't know what the fuck they're doing. My biggest fear is getting myself beaten up ... I want to go home in one piece. I have a family, a girlfriend to go home to. If there are thirty guys there who want to drink and party, I'll back down, you know: 'OK guys you win, we're leaving.' But then I'll be back with seven guys and four dogs to disperse them. There's no point trying to be a hero and getting your head kicked in every night. (mobile security officer – male)

Pre-emptive back-up is not an uncommon practice among the parapolice. Perhaps the best-known form of it, which the company sanctions, is trespass interdiction programs (TIPs). TIPs are basically round-ups of multiple suspects using many security officers and guard dogs. In a TIP, drug dealers, trespassers, and offenders are arrested simultaneously in a single sweep of a building, lobby, or other structure:

They just did a TIP recently. We get five or six guys in a van and closed in on them. The property was slipping, and we didn't have the presence there that we would have liked so in we go. Everybody was notified ahead of time. I'm not sure how the billing works. (mobile security officer – male)

If we ever perform any special duties or special TIPs we try to inform them [property managers] first. They don't like surprises. (mobile security officer – male)

A TIP is intended to dissuade drug dealers, prostitutes, and other 'undesirables' from conducting their business on Intelligarde-secured properties. Intelligarde maintains that in making it harder for offenders to sell their merchandise on its sites, it is simply driving those offenders to other locations.

Whatever their rationale, TIPs are in effect swarmings orchestrated by the Law Enforcement Company. The planning of 'official' TIPs involves site surveillance and the videotaping of suspects before collective action is launched. With the consent of the property owner, ten or more Intelligarde officers descend on a site in vans with guard dogs, and arrest predetermined suspects congregating in lobby areas or clear squatters from crack houses (see *Toronto Star*, 25 August 1989: A7; *Toronto Life*, April 1995: 53, 55–58; *Toronto Star*, 9 August 1989: A1; *Toronto Star*, 6 August 1989: A7). Often these actions are highly visible and are greeted with cheers from residents. They are also highly dangerous and often brutal. Suspects and Intelligarde officers are regularly injured in these altercations. These interventions intimidate Intelligarde's enemies because they are swift, brutal, and unexpected.

Less talked about are unsanctioned TIPs mustered by security officers without management's approval. After the swarming involving J, Intelligarde management decided that reprisals would only escalate matters. Frustrated by the MTP's inability to bring the offenders to justice, a few Intelligarde leaders orchestrated an informal TIP of their own. This involved gathering up six officers and a few dogs for a patrol in force of the site. All of the officers took time out from their patrol runs to get involved. The deployment did not produce an altercation, but it was important for symbolic purposes. As one veteran mobile security officer put it, 'Nothing happened, but if we saw any of those guys ourselves, we would have taken them down.' But as it happened, 'there was no way they'd poke their noses around there so soon after the incident. I know that their friends and look-outs got the word back to them that we were there looking for them, and that's enough.'

Intelligarde security officers are always trying to muster more people more quickly than the enemy. This is true whether these mobilizations are official or unofficial. So it is no wonder that the parapolice call for assistance before attempting an arrest in a public area or in other circumstances that might elicit collective resistance. Mobilization records for 1997 show that there is a statistically significant difference in the mean number of officers responding to incidents involving the public police or arrests, relative to incidents in which the police were not called or no arrest ensued. In situations where arrests were made or the police called, the average number of officers present was significantly greater (see Table 6.1). To a certain extent, these findings are hardly surprising. It is only logical that more officers would respond to more volatile incidents. But when these statistical findings are wedded to the ethnographic observations presented earlier, a picture emerges of serendipitous TIPs and swarmings that are tantamount to what has elsewhere been termed 'fire brigade policing' (Smith and Gray, 1983). In effect, these findings support the conclusion that a 'swarm or be swarmed' occupational ethic insists that invariably breeds fear, uneasiness, and perpetual reliance on mutual assistance.

TABLE 6.1
The Relationship between arrests, police presence, and security officer response

Mean no. of S/Os		t
Police		
Yes	2.00	
(n = 128)		9.558***
No	1.21	
(n = 210)		df = 336
Arrest		
Yes	1.75	
(n = 110)		3.756***
No	1.39	
(n = 230)		df = 338

***p < .001
Based on systematic random sample (n = 340) of
company occurrence report files (N = 1,703) (at
95% confidence interval, p = .05, precision =
±5%). S/Os = security officers. 'Arrest' also
includes detained persons issued NPEs.

In his history of the French Foreign Legion (1986), Tony Geraghty described the mercenary lore of the *Regiment Étrangerès* as fostering a fierce regimental loyalty. Considered not quite as good as France's 'true' army, looked down upon by many Frenchmen and political figures, and deployed in the most hostile (and often suicidal) theatres of war because they are 'expendable,' legionnaires have had to look within themselves to construct some meaning for their existence. At the obvious risk of romanticizing the monotony of security work in Toronto's underbelly, I find a similar ethos among Intelligarde's men and women. Often looked down upon by the public, attacked by angry mobs, treated with indifference or disdain by the state's 'true' police, and asked to patrol areas where most would not tread, Intelligarde security officers can look only to one another for support.

On the other hand, fear and group solidarity often have negative effects. In explaining why police officers respond differently to various members of the public, Skolnick (1966) refers to the construction of 'symbolic assailants.' A person whose clothes and mannerisms suggest that he or she will cause trouble is more likely to be treated harshly. The subculture teaches officers how to identify dangerous situations. Stories of resistance – or in the case of Intelligarde, swarmings – foster a cultural narrative of the 'typical' violence-prone suspect. For Intelligarde officers this is clearly a young black man, usually of Jamaican descent. On one level, these perceptions are merely the product of doing police work – one makes decisions on the basis of past experience, both individual and organizational. As one Intelligarde manager put it, 'Your longevity is based on your ability to apply labels.' On another level, however, a predetermined course of action based on the 'look' or skin colour of a suspect is clearly prejudicial and smacks of systemic racism, whatever the rationale.

It is not surprising to learn that Intelligarde security dogs have a reputation for lunging at black people:

People sometimes say to us, 'You train your dogs to hate black people.' My answer to that is, 'No we don't, they train themselves.' We never train our dogs to react on the basis of clothing or skin colour or anything like that. Our dogs are there to protect the security officer. If the officer is tense or roused, so is the dog ... In this business, dogs quickly become systemic racists because they don't have to rationalize their actions, they act out of instinct and past experience. (Intelligarde manager)

Much like their handlers, the dogs have been socialized – often through indirect cues – to react to particular populations in particular ways. When the handler is roused, so is the dog that is trained to protect him or her.

This chapter has discussed resistance and subcultural mores among the Intelligarde parapolice. As I expected, I found multiple modes of resistance operating in opposition to the techniques of hyperpanoptic control delineated in Chapter 5. The disciplining techniques employed by management have counterproductive and unforeseen consequences among the general guard force. Tied to our knowledge of parapolice resistance is an appreciation for the subcultural priorities that shape it. Crime fighting and the wannabe culture, as well as the environment of limitless risks that must be policed, breed uneasiness and the urge to maintain a strong albeit unofficial strategy of collective resistance. The result is the dialectic reproduction of more threats and fear, among both the populations being policed and the parapolice themselves.

Closing Remarks

It was near the end of my time in the field that I was escorted over to a property in the Intelligarde territory of St James Town. As we walked toward the site, I noticed that the evening pedestrian traffic on this private roadway was strangely polarized. For some reason only the south sidewalk was being used, but many people were idling about the lobby and front entrance on the north side. When I came to the Intelligarde building, I asked the site officer why nobody was congregating about their property but at least twenty people were on the other side of the roadway. The simple answer, according to him, was that the building opposite was not secured by Intelligarde.

As I sat on a landscape wall, the Intelligarde officer looked over to the other building as he puffed on a cigarette. As far as he was concerned, the 'dealers' would not dare ply their trade on his side of the street as long as he was on duty. We sat under a No Loitering sign that empowered site security officers to arrest for 'prohibited' activity on their patch. A few minutes later, an older woman who was walking her dog came across the street to strike up a conversation. I stopped my interview and listened to her ask the security officer what a handgun laser sight looked like. She reported that while walking behind the other building, someone had shone a red dot on her leg and on her dog. This terrified her. The woman began complaining that she could not even walk her dog without fear of being shot. The security officer asked her to report the incident to the Housing Authority security, because he was not responsible for the property in question. The woman moaned that they would not do anything for her and said she would call the police.

Soon after that, two other women came across to us to report the same occurrence. Again, the security officer asked them to report the incident to MTHA security, but this only prompted the women to deride the MTHA personnel as 'scared.' 'They're not like you guys,' one woman added. 'They're afraid to approach these guys. When are you going to come to our buildings?' The security officer smiled and said, 'Talk to your tenant's association.' Is this the future of policing? Territorially bounded contract policing services for hire? A series of organizations poised to fill the emotional and material voids of security in emerging risk markets? In this final chapter, I review the theoretical assumptions, research questions, and central findings I have presented in this book, and discuss some of the political implications of this research.

On Theory

My analysis has been guided by four ideas about the 'selling' of risk. *First*, a risk markets orientation recognizes that contract private policing is centrally alienated and commodified labour. The modern organization of policing can best be understood in this way. The early, duty-bound organization of policing gave way to policing for profit (the commercial compromise of the state) as soon as the mode of production that governed policing mutated from feudalism to capitalism. If new actuarial logics have come to govern policing institutions, how are these knowledges sold back to the consumer? In this book I have analysed police work as knowledge work for sale – as a management system for hire.

Second, 'risk society' and the 'fetishisms of security' are inherently political phenomena. A risk markets perspective strongly questions the recent trend in 'risk society' social theory that uncritically accepts how populations under institutional surveillance are organized and categorized. This is a regrettable neo-Weberian tendency. Sociologists have correctly identified the organizing logics and institutional rationales of risk systems, but have failed to offer perceptive critiques of these schemas (cf. Rigakos, 1999a). They have uncritically adopted these productions of knowledge as the actual organizers of society instead of revealing their legitimating functions in late modern capitalism. These processes are thus reified, as if the corporate-managerial epistemes that fuelled them are self-evident, transparent, and in no further need of inquiry. Often, this propensity is masked by the (misused) Foucauldian project of the archaeology of knowledge (or the history of the present), which supposedly sheds its critical incubus by making such political positionings extraneous to its project (O'Malley, 2001). A risk markets perspective places the political process of ordering populations at the forefront of its analysis. We cannot understand the policing of Jamaicans in west North York merely by analysing managerial procedures and deployment practices. Supposedly, these are cold and calculated decisions that ostensibly do not have a political motivation (Rigakos, 1998). Yet in the eyes of the security officers meant to police that territory and of the people being policed, the process is nothing if not political.

Third, given the commodified nature of both public and private policing, there is little justification for differentiating the missions of these two institutions (Rigakos, 2000; see also Johnston, 1992). This is a dated assumption that the public and private police have fundamentally divergent goals: that the public police concern themselves with controlling criminal activity and especially physical harm to people, whereas the private police are tasked with preventing theft of or damage to property. These orienting logics are described as either 'loss prevention' or 'crime prevention' missions (Shearing and Stenning, 1982b; 1983). More recently, academic thinking has begun to change (e.g., Kempa et al., 1999) to account for the multiple uses and manifestations of contract private security (and private policing more generally). However, it is still implicitly (sometimes explicitly) assumed that the new police in structure and purpose are essentially 'new' or 'post-Keynesian' (O'Malley and Palmer, 1996). In other words, that the 'rebirth' of private policing is somehow a fundamentally different phenomenon from what is happening in public policing. That this change is a result of 'new' thinking that cannot but lead to completely new ways to organize safety – usually along the lines of actuarial models such as 'responsibilization' and loss prevention (Shearing, 2000). In this book I have challenged this assumption by providing both observational and statistical evidence which demonstrates – at least in the case of Intelligarde – that the role of the modern private police often closely resembles the role of the first private constabularies in eighteenth-century England, and mirrors the aspirations and functions of the contemporary public police.

Both ethnographic and statistical data support this assertion. The logics of the private and public police are interchangeable largely because both forms of security provision are at least representationally commodified under capitalism. Thus, *private* and *public* can refer to little more than the official designations of the policing service in question – and this tells us very little about their operations. Perhaps state and corporate police services are behaving in increasingly similar ways, and crowding each other for the same risk markets, simply because their roles are so similar under unfettered late capitalism. If Intelligarde's management gets its way, its parapolice will soon acquire special constabulary or provincial offences officer status. This will make the already muddled distinctions between 'private' and 'public' even more meaningless. And this only further reveals their inherently analogous 'commodified' nature. The *only real alternatives to current policing practices, therefore, are pre-capitalist, non-commodified security arrangements* whereby each citizen is duty-bound to protect his or her own collective. Under a system like this, the labour of security produces no 'surplus-value' and each individual who provides such labour constitutes his or her own 'natural production unit' (Marx, 1972: 130–9). This approach is found today in uncompensated citizen patrols and in vigilantism. Only in this way does the fundamental organization of security provision materially transform itself. Otherwise, the nature of security provision is characterized by the selling of commodified social control to fear-induced risk markets – in many instances for profit.

In rhetoric and reality, the parapolice of Toronto are private law enforcement officers who have been hired to 'control crime' rather than merely to minimize risk. Perhaps my claims are not so controversial, given that contemporary police theorists and researchers are becoming more and more likely to concede that the 'traditional public/private dichotomy has ... lost a great deal of its salience in characterizing developments in the process of policing and the organization of collective life' (Kempa et al., 1999: 219).

Fourth and finally, a risk markets orientation examines the processes of both surveillance and resistance in private policing in a dialectic of control. New 'governmentality' discourses and their correlative applications to the study of policing institutions reduce officers to mere automatons (Ericson, 1994; Ericson and Haggerty, 1997; Ericson, Haggerty, and Carriere, 1993). This mode of investigation privileges paper realities and organizational schemas at the expense of the actors imagined as falling within their purview. Classic studies in the sociology of policing focused almost exclusively on the occupational culture of line officers (e.g., Manning, 1997; Skolnick, 1966; Westley, 1970). These subcultural approaches have had a long and distinguished history in criminological inquiry since being imported from anthropology by Albert Cohen (1955). Subcultural theory assumes that social life is guided and regulated by shared values and norms and that these values and norms are different from those of the broader society. These shared values are a product of the group's similar aversive subjective experiences – such as status frustration – which can be directly traced to the group's social location. Deviant behaviour in the subculture is learned and diffused as collective, problem-solving behaviour.

At the beginning of Chapter 2, I distilled two central questions from the perspective I proffered in the theoretical set-up for this book. Before I answer these questions from the information I have gathered, we need to take stock of the theoretical assumptions that produced them.

Risk markets are cyclical, and produce a constant spiral of fears, along with the need to manage them. The very act of securing properties and people visibly and concretely reinforces this reproducing pattern: more security breeds more insecurity. This is most clearly seen in the dialectic of TIPs and swarmings between the parapolice and subject populations. Much like the public police, the Intelligarde parapolice produce information about risky populations, which they gather through the disciplining practices of surveillance. These practices are politically charged and contested when applied to the chaotic environments they are meant to order. It is no coincidence that 35 per cent of individuals banned from properties secured by Intelligarde are homeless, and that the people most likely to engage the parapolice in street brawls are young West Indian males. The actuarial practices of policing can hardly avoid perpetuating present inequities.

In answer to the two orienting questions for this book, therefore, the short answers become rather obvious:

1. *How are discipline and surveillance achieved organizationally and sold externally to risk markets?* Through the process of surveillance embedded in the actual act of symbolically producing commodified security. The very techniques that the Law Enforcement Company utilizes for amassing information about suspect populations and for controlling its own workforce are depicted in a digitally encoded 'product' for the client. These techniques include both the 'Deister' management system and the production of reporting formats (and the knowledge this elicits).
2. *How do security agents and those they are tasked with policing resist social control?* By means of the very techniques and virtual templates of social control constructed by managers. While electronic checkpoints, video surveillance, and the constant monitoring of security officers may imply total control within a digitally pre-figured workplace, the reality described in this book is quite different. For almost every technique of hyperpanoptic management, there exists a means

of circumvention. Intelligarde officers have developed many inge-
nious methods to 'ghost' their presence within artificial, digital representations of their labour. As a result, managers must purchase
even more comprehensive tools of surveillance, or develop additional techniques to discipline their staff in a dialectic of control. On
a much less nuanced level of resistance, the parapolice themselves
are forced to confront groups of suspects, who often physically attack
and collectively defend themselves.

Finally, it must be emphasized again that the subculture of the parapolice (as with the public police) plays a vital role in defining occupational
rules and organizational mobilizations.

Future Research

Despite some impressive accomplishments by the Toronto school (i.e.,
Shearing and Stenning et al.), and despite large-scale American survey
research (e.g., Hallcrest, Rand), the sociology of private policing is still
in its infancy. Many areas of exploration are still open. Admittedly,
'more research is needed' is an academic cliché, but private policing
affects social organization and the legitimacy of government so directly
that we have no choice but to continue concerted empirical investigations at the macro and micro levels. For example, almost nothing has
been written about night club 'bouncers,' who exercise violence routinely and are very likely to be victimized themselves. They are a form of
private police (usually unproductive in-house labour operating at a loss
to revenue) with a distinct culture and history and with particular relationships to public order in the night-time economy (Hobbs and Hall,
2000; Lister et al., 1999). Even more importantly, there have been no systematic attempts (their lack of recent fashion notwithstanding) to posit
some general theory or general laws on the relationship between public
and private policing. This could well be worthwhile in the context of
political economy, inequality, and Marxist theory, especially in light of
the proliferation of transnational corporate security entities and local
gated communities. It is time to research 'glocally.'
    What this means is not some fundamental shift in thinking so much as
specific attention to the most salient aspects of contract private security
– the fact that it is a business and obeys the laws of the market. This is
what this book has largely attempted to invoke. Contract security firms
are everywhere, doing both low-level and highly skilled police work. The

Intelligarde parapolice may be satisfied with providing second-tier policing; in contrast, private forensic accounting firms and corporate investigators conduct complete higher-order internal investigations before
turning information over to the less capable public police. Often run
and staffed by experienced police managers, the constellation of interactions between firms such as FIA Inc. and KPMG with the public police
will be qualitatively different from those described for Intelligarde and
GTA police services. More research is also needed on these specialized
and often secretive organizations. Having reconsidered this books' theoretical assertions and overviewed some possible directions for future
research, let us now consider the political implications of some of the
trends I have identified.

On Governance

If it were up to anarcho-libertarians like Friedman (1973) and Rothbard
(1978), both the provision of policing and the law itself would be little
more than products in a system of laissez-faire competition. The best
police, the most popular, would be the most successful, the most profitable. People should have the ability to choose between a multiplicity of
police services, as they now do between bras or books. If you wanted to
ban alcohol, you would buy a strip of land and ban it there. If you wanted
to outlaw loitering, you would hire a law enforcement company to
enforce these provisions. There is little doubt that the organization of
policing is historically and politically contingent. It is no coincidence
that the recent amendments to the Police Services Act in Ontario that
make it possible for private firms to enter into competitions for tertiary
policing duties were implemented by a neoconservative regime. It is also
not surprising to find Intelligarde's president Ross McLeod quoting liberal economic dogma in support of his attempts to sell his security product to institutions, corporations, and even the public police. On 12
January 1999, he sent out a circular to all Ontario municipal police chiefs
itemizing, in economic terms, why they should speak to him about contracting some services from Intelligarde. McLeod also made a presentation before the Standing Committee on the Administration of Justice
(Tuesday, 18 March 1997) in regard to amending the Police Services Act
in this manner. He argued that private police agencies should be
granted a limited range of powers to supplement public police services.
Of course, the New Democratic Party (social democrats) representative
from Hamilton Centre, David Christopherson, was resistant to the idea:

Mr Christopherson:	Thank you for your presentation. Before I comment, to be fair, I'm not real keen on the idea of the proliferation of private policing as we're seeing in the States. I offer that up front, before I ask my questions. You said it's cost-effective. The first question is: Are you proposing that these officers would have the full powers of a police officer?
Mr McLeod:	No. You can have a range, from the powers we largely now [*sic*], which are no additional powers to the average citizen of the age of majority, right up to special constable status. The special constable status can be a warrant limited to a time, a place, while in uniform, working for a named company, and only for a listed number of offences, for instance, noise bylaw, environmental, stoop and scoop, that sort of thing. It can be delimited to a very, very set number of low-level offences.
Mr Christopherson:	It can be similar to a security guard, so clearly not offering private policing per se, which is the impression that was certainly left with me.
Mr McLeod:	I think 'private policing' is an unfortunate name that summons up all sorts of different images with different people. What we're talking about here is a sort of value-added security service; it's a bylaw enforcement service; it's community-based policing. I'm not talking about a totally privatised law enforcement effort, as we see in small American communities where the police force is totally privatised. I'm talking to a para-police function that assists and segues into and is used by the public police who still maintain their exclusive access to all Criminal Code enforcement.
Mr Christopherson:	I think the concern is that it's a slippery slope.

Social democratic governments (and parties such as the NDP) would be hard-pressed to justify such measures.[1] Indeed, critical policing experts such as the Left Realist school in Britain have repeatedly sought to make local police more accountable (see Currie, DeKeseredy, and MacLean, 1992, for a review). These initiatives have revolved around the production of knowledge about crime and the resultant community interest this galvanizes – including among the police themselves. Local crime surveys have gathered data about fear levels, victimization, and attitudes toward the police as part of attempts to make the public police answerable to the community. These initiatives have had only limited success (Currie, DeKeseredy, and MacLean, 1992: 293) in selected locales. After decades of critical scholarship and public outcries about the lack of police accountability in Western democracies, the status quo has hardly changed. Crime prevention, much like loss prevention, can be purchased and is no longer a monopoly of the modern state. Communities can buy confrontational or 'social' policing (Intelligarde or MTHA) as a function of their needs (Carder, 1994). This requires us to reassess our current understandings of private policing and community. Both contracts are dynamic and multifaceted; neither lends itself easily to definitive assertions. Some private policing agencies engage in activities similar to those of the public police, and these agencies are either vilified or glorified depending on which 'community' you query. Who belongs to the tenant association? Who are its enemies? Critical scholars have long levelled these questions at public police agencies and recent community-based policing rhetorics, so it is not surprising to find them resurfacing as private police organizations take on the functions of the public police. How will private police organizations be accountable? Are the current mechanisms comprehensive enough, or will new forms of accountability need to be implemented as the private police become more involved in crime control and private law enforcement? Is the market the best mode of accountability? Who will the private police be answerable to? What is the community? Are the rate payer, the landowner, the tenant, the merchant, and the trespasser equally capable of obtaining redress? All these questions become increasingly important as forensic accounting firms and corporate security services take on responsibility for private actions that are also Criminal Code offences.

Perhaps the greatest irony here is that the strongest assault against public policing as an institution has been mounted by neoliberal ideology. Nils Christie (1993) has argued that the rise of the private police result in two classes of policing – one for the affluent, and the other for the poor. Of course, Christie is only partly correct here: as we have seen, companies such as Intelligarde often work for the working poor, and their hourly rates are much higher than the industry standard. When they police their fellow proletariat (or lumpen-), this complicates (though it need not negate) Marxian theory.[2] The researcher is forced to consider much more than a simplistic class abstraction, including commodity fetishism, the power of purchasing collectives, and even false consciousness, and racism. Christie continues:

> If the Gestapo and the KGB had been branches of a private firm, hired by
> dictators, they might have been equally efficient and ugly in their methods,
> but would not to the same extent have intimidated their state régimes.
> When parts of the crime control system belong to the state, there is at least
> some hope that those parts will be destroyed when the state is destroyed ...
> But if they are private, they are even more protected when the régime falls.
> (Christie, 1993: 109)

Christie offers evidence that private organizations continued to support
Nazism through research, armaments, and so on after the collapse of
the Third Reich. The firms that produced equipment for the concentra-
tion camps and used prisoners as slave labour continue to prosper in
Germany today. Many of them are now 'transnational' organizations.

The very political economy that the state police services supported so
fervently in the past may ultimately bring down the public police in its
present form. The biggest challenge to the present organization of
policing will come not from Marxist and liberal thinkers who want a professional, public, representative, and accountable service, but rather
from the capitalist zealots that the police have historically protected by
smashing labour unrest and by subverting labour organizations through
agents provocateurs. The great irony here is that the public police's last
great appeal for legitimacy may have to be aimed at the social democrats
and critics they have attacked throughout their history. Who else will lis-
ten to their belated discovery of 'public good,' equity, and the safety and
security of all citizens? At the recent, and first ever, National Conference
on Police and Security, held in Toronto in November 1999, those few
criminologists in attendance could not help but chortle as they listened
to police union leaders extol the virtues of accountability, transparency,
professionalism, and so on in the face of a perceived threat from private
security. Perhaps we are witnessing the development of another series of
circumlocutions. In any case, critical theorists are torn about all of this:
creeping or unfettered capitalism according to the neoliberal dogma of
'open markets' and consumerism could easily result in a feudal collage
of private police organizations serving no other purpose except to valo-
rize capital around the globe. On the one hand, we could say 'so be it'
and applaud the unmasking of risk markets under laissez-faire capitalism. After all, the police, be they public or private, have always been
about the protection of those with property and assets to the exclusion
of others. The façade of 'public good' has only hidden this fact. On the
other hand, we could work within these fracturing risk markets to create

collective policing (or social caretaking) as an alternative socialist framework (à la New Left Realism, etc.). Under creeping capitalism, consumers are now demanding that policing be demystified. They want to know precisely where their tax dollars are going, since those dollars apparently give them more power now under neoliberalism – or so it would seem. By this logic, however, the bigger the taxpayer, the louder the voice! Can reform ever be achieved through this mechanism, or will this corporatist rhetoric serve only to kill the idea of police? These are profound political questions, which I have barely touched in this book.

Usually, at this stage of a book, the researcher turns to the immediate issue of his or her object of analysis and offers some entreaty about police policy, invariably: more training, more accountability, heightened sensitivity toward the poor, the development of understanding about racial diversity, and so on. All of this is valid, I am sure, but I am more interested in how we understand the parapolice than in writing policy to curb their activities or the activities of other security firms. This is now even more true because of the renewed interest by public police unions in further regulating the security industry – much to the chagrin of Intelligarde. When one believes, as I do, that this is merely the posturing of competing security organizations jockeying for position in potential risk markets, one hardly finds it palatable acting as referee. There are just as many reforms needed in public policing, perhaps more. This is yet one more reason why 'policing' must be viewed as a general activity, and reform or revolution aimed at its totality.

Notes

Introduction

1 It turned out that the man in the arm sling had been injured while being arrested for punching and breaking a window and for being intoxicated on private property. The security officer in question is no longer with the company.

2 In this study the reader is taken through a trip to Disneyland. During each moment of enjoyment, the authors draw attention to the many ways in which social control is unobtrusively maintained, albeit the agents themselves are not analysed in this manner.

1: Theorizing the Private Police

1 This does not include the sizeable in-house security guard population.

2 Including agencies involved in early American strike-breaking, which continue to operate (e.g., Pinkerton's) or latter-day firms such as Vance & Wackenhut.

3 Instead of focusing on the state and labour, Klare (1975) likened postwar private security firms in an era of McCarthyism to 'private C.I.A.s' that colluded with state interests in amassing information on organizations and people deemed a security threat to the establishment. But his account did not adequately explain why this information was kept, or its purpose. For Klare, it was insidious enough that such materials were amassed at all. Klare's piece implies that the private police are part of an agenda to undermine progressive politics. See also the work of Gary Marx and Nancy Reichman (1988) on computers as informants.

4 A slightly different interpretation has been offered by Johnson (1976) who

makes race central to his sociohistoric account. Johnson argues that labour in the eastern American cities has struck a relationship of solidarity with the public police. This alliance promotes a 'legitimating' atmosphere of persecution against cheap black labour. Blacks are kept out of the labour pool through arrest and stigmatization; meanwhile, whites enjoy wage and job security. Public and private police routinely trade criminal record information, and this restricts black people's access to the job market. Élites have repeatedly tried to 'professionalize' the police, but according to Johnson this challenges both police and popular sensibilities regarding the function of the constabulary as an intervening line between the proletariat (whites) and the lumpenproletariat (blacks).

5 One notable exception is Canada's quasi-public Corps of Commissioners, who have a 'right of first refusal' on all government buildings and who do not operate to realize a profit. Interestingly, the Corps has recently begun a for-profit branch called 'Corps 2.'

6 In a letter written to Engels when he was nearly finished his manuscript of *Capital*, Marx said that he intended his project to comprise six books, the fourth of which was to focus on the state. We are all the more theoretically impoverished by the fact that this treatise was never written (Nicolaus, 1973: 54).

7 In fact, much of Intelligarde's client base depends upon such arrangements.

8 These tenant's associations pay for their policing services indirectly through their rent – both public and private.

2: Methods of Inquiry

1 Such approaches have been described elsewhere as attempts at 'triangulation' (Denzin 1978) – a series of methods utilized to limit the margin of error or inaccuracy when only one investigative tool is employed.

2 My thanks to Stephanie Duncan at the *Toronto Star* switchboard for her assistance.

3 Refers to a scheduled visit and patrol of a site lasting between 30 and 50 minutes.

4 Based on field note entries.

5 Most of the fieldwork also involved audiotaping respondents. I transcribed these recordings soon after. This allowed me to use the tapes in future interviews.

6 Researchers have distributed surveys to Ontario (Shearing, Farnell, and Stenning 1980) and Toronto (Erickson 1993) security officers, but the research instruments did not query them about attitudes.

7 Representing the following firms: Intelligarde International, Metropol Secu-

rity (West Toronto), Intercon Security, Wackenhut Security, Metropol Security (East Toronto), Burns Security, Pinkerton's (Canadian HQ – Montreal), Pinkerton's (Toronto), Group 4 Securitas, and Fidelity Alarms.

8 The original study targeted respondents who worked for companies that:

- offer innovative security products such as complete vertical product and service integration; or
- hold high-profile contracts that were once within the realm of the public sector; or
- are part of large multinational security syndicates engaged in private correctional services, public purview policing (such as court security and prisoner transport), or consulting on the reformation of former Eastern Bloc police services; or
- maintain a high-profile guard force trained in self-defence and/or dog handling, who are instructed to make arrests, or who are engaged in other non-customary security functions.

I make no claims about the representativeness of this study's sample. For instance, private policing outfits such as forensic accounting firms and other 'high end' corporate security companies may constitute another level of policing activity (e.g., KPMG, FIA Inc., Deloitte Touche, and Public Safety Innovation).

9 Job placement for 2 of the 141 employees could not be obtained.

10 I will discuss this – and the subcultural mores of Intelligarde officers generally – in greater detail in upcoming chapters.

11 Since Intelligarde has received considerable media attention of late, some veteran security officers treated my inquiries as routine. It was clear that they had been interviewed and taped by the media in the past.

12 The occurrence reports were shuffled to avoid systematic sampling bias due to Intelligarde's procedure of organizing the files by site. A six-sided die was rolled, and every fifth file thereafter was selected until 340 were picked.

13 They have changed often in the last few years.

14 This proved quite difficult because there was a lack of standardization in the 'date of offence' field. Often, months and days were variably ordered which made it nearly impossible to tell if an NPE had been issued on, for example, 10 January or 1 October. However, since NPEs were often entered chronologically, I was able to make some judgments about their inclusion in the sample.

15 There are probably just as many individuals banned from Intelligarde sites informally – warnings are given and no paperwork ensues.

3: The New Parapolice

1 Since the writing of this chapter, many of the security arrangements and contractors at the airport have changed.

2 MTHA has its own in-house security – many officers have the power to issue provincial offences tickets. They are, in effect, provincial offences officers.

3 *Displacement* refers to the direct effect that police (or other) interventions have in shifting criminal activity to another area rather than actually stopping it (see Gabor, 1981).

4 A similar arrangement is in place in the Borough of Southwark, England. In that council estate, private security is employed to conduct low-level drug enforcement. The security guards report to twenty local councillors, a local community tenants' representative, a neighbourhood housing office, and community safety coordinators (Lee 1991).

5 In England they have a much more pronounced role as functioning auxiliaries to the public police (Johnston, 1992: 140–6).

6 I am referring here to the Eaton Centre, the Jane-Finch Mall, and Dufferin Mall.

7 As in the case of Intelligarde's Cabbagetown properties.

8 They have trademarked this phrase.

9 When a particular omission or negligent act is observed that places people or property at risk, the security officer leaves a form (snowflake) aimed at bringing the potentially risky situation to the attention of the employee and management. Habitual violators are thus tracked, and reprimands can be issued. An example of a violation might be leaving a portable computer unsecured.

10 This is buttressed by assertions made by both Intelligarde and other security executives. Indeed, except for licensing, there are scant grounds for comparison but umpteen points of contrast.

11 A person can also be banned from certain sections of a private property but not from others. This is typically done under section 4(2) of the Trespass to Property Act.

12 The authors cite *Dillon* v. *O'Brien* (1887) 17 Cox C.C. 245, at pp. 249–50, and *Reynen* v. *Antonenko et al.* (1975) 30 C.R.N.S. 135. For post–Constitution Act rulings, see Hoskins (1997) and *Cloutier* v. *Langlois* (1990), 53 C.C.C. (3d) 257 S.C.C., where the court spelled out that searches can be conducted on persons incidental to arrest in order to secure objects that may be used in evidence, weapons that may be a threat to public safety, or objects that may aid in escape. See also Rigakos and Greener (2000).

13 According to the respondent, there are approximately 1,000 commissioners

in the greater Toronto area. A commissioner is usually represented by a law firm and is sworn in by the lieutenant-governor.

14 Shearing (1997) contends that the origins of the new community policing rhetorics may, in fact, be located within the growth of private security. This challenges contemporary policing arrangements. For a comprehensive review of community-based policing evaluations, see Rigakos (1997a).

15 The 1996 Annual Report does not contain the same level statistical exposition provided in the previous year. I could not obtain the same tables presented in the 1995 Statistics Companion to the Annual Report from MTP Corporate Communications. In any case, a 7.2 per cent drop in Criminal Code offences from 1995 to 1996 in Toronto means that 1995 statistics for the MTP (Metropolitan Toronto Police Service 1996:28) may be comparatively inflated in Table 3.1. This makes the resultant similarities with Intelligarde even more remarkable.

16 All of which began with private informations.

17 The rationale for these dismissals included unauthorized use of computer equipment, sleeping on the job, and warning other officers that a supervisor was in the area.

18 This is an estimate based on the 4,560 alarm responses in the alarm database. 'System crashes' resulted in five months of missing or partial information so that only twenty-one months of data were deemed reliable. At 7.2 dispatches per night, interpolations suggest that Intelligarde dispatches approximately 2,628 alarm responses per year. According to one communications officer, however, this figure may be a conservative calculation. The respondent noted: 'On a Monday we may have five but on a Saturday we may have up to twenty.' The other problem with such an estimate is that Intelligarde's alarm response business has reportedly grown in the last year.

19 A used soda pop can is intentionally dented on the end opposite to the drinking hole so that the user can rest a crack rock on it for cooking. The indented area is punctured to allow the fumes to be sucked through the can and out the spout for inhaling.

20 Double-spent matches mean two matches torn from a match casing and burnt simultaneously. Apparently, this provides the optimum heat necessary to liquify and make gaseous the methamphetamine 'rock' for inhaling.

21 Parking Authority of Toronto car. An Intelligarde security vehicle exclusively devoted to patrolling Toronto's public parking lots. It is equipped with an on-board camera.

22 Mentally ill.

23 An electronic patrol checkpoint. More on this in chapters 4 and 5.

24 One's position (or 'indexicality') governs one's perceptions. I wonder how

terrified I would be if I was a sleeping homeless man and a group of uniformed men broke through the darkness, silhouetted only by their scanning flashlights: 'Objects exist only in relation to the interpretative meaning they have for the people who behold them' (Pfohl, 1985: 294, referring to the work of ethnomethodologists).

4: Inside a Law Enforcement Company

1 I was introduced to the incoming class by the trainer on the first day. It was easy to ask questions of the recruits because they were the ones who actually initiated contact – asking me about my purpose and my perceptions of the company. They were as eager to know about Intelligarde as I was to know about them. My presence may have further legitimized Intelligarde's parapolicing program in the eyes of the recruits. It is not often that security companies are studied by a university researchers.

2 The number of cases in the personnel files for which information about previous employment is available.

3 Since the writing of this book, and in part as a result of Intelligarde management having read it, a non-cellular single-frequency radio system has been reintroduced.

4 This is also true of non-residential spaces. In North York's notorious Jane-Finch Mall, security officers are leery of arresting black suspects in the open. The preferred tactic is to isolate them by asking to 'talk' in a more private setting. Here, an arrest can ensue. Otherwise, the arresting officer calls for assistance in advance of the arrest so that three or four security personnel are available to dissuade public involvement. Of course, this can inadvertently result in a display of overwhelming force in the face of a rather insignificant offence such as shoplifting.

5 *R. v. Chraba and Huyton* (1997) Ont. Unreported, p. 3.

6 Ibid., p. 4.

7 Caution should be exercised with this finding, however, because three cells (16.7 per cent) had expected cell counts of less than 5. The minimum expected count was 3.95. This 2×2 table fails DeLucchi's (1983) amended Lewis and Burke goodness-of-fit standards. See footnote 8 for more information.

8 There are 211 cases for which complexion, race, or ethnic characteristics are not listed.

9 In the 2×2 χ-square cross-tabulation for gender, one cell (25 per cent) had an expected count of less than 5. The minimum expected count is 2.77. In the 2×2 χ-square cross-tabulation for race, 0 cells had an expected count of less

than 5. The minimum expected count is 8.24. To test the veracity of the tables, I employed DeLucchi's (1983) amended Lewis and Burke goodness-of-fit standards. He noted: 'Summarizing this work on minimum expected values for both association and goodness-of-fit hypotheses, it seems that, as a general rule, the chi-square statistic may be properly used in cases where the expected values are much lower than previously considered permissible. In the presence of small expected values, the statistic is quite robust with respect to controlling Type 1 error rate, especially under the following conditions: (a) the total N is at least five times the number of cells, (b) the average expected value is five or more, (c) the expected values tend toward homogeneity, and (d) the distribution of the margins is not skewed' (Delucchi 1983: 168).

5: A Parapolice Surveillance System

1 See ch. 3, n. 9.
2 Or commercial.
3 This is a name brand for an electronic patrol checkpoint system.
4 One communications officer was upset to see me analysing the various databases and files, because this threatened a planned reinstatement of the crime analyst position, which he was in line to fill.
5 For a discussion of productive and unproductive labour, see Mandel (1975), Carchedi (1977), Leadbeater (1985), and Kushnirsky and Stull (1989), or go to the originals (Smith, 1937; Marx, 1972b). There has also been some more consideration of the productivity issue for criminology (see Hirst, 1973; 1975).

6: Solidarity, Fear, and Subculture

1 At this stage in English policing, it was common for constables to be paid replacements for more affluent citizens. Typically, many justices of the peace and marshalls (as in the case of Jonathan Wild) ran private thief-taking organizations alongside their public duties.
2 Trespass interdiction program.

Closing Remarks

1 See Johnston (1992: 24–44) for a thoughtful examination of the links between private and public state functionings and their correlative political rationales.
2 See Reiner (1978; 1992) for an interesting consideration of police in the class structure.

References

Baudrillard, Jean. 1983. *Simulations.* New York: Semiotext(e).

Bayley, David H. 1988. 'Community policing.' Pp. 225–38 in *Community Policing: Rhetoric or Reality?* edited by Jack R. Greene and Stephen D. Mastroski. New York: Praeger.

Bayley, David H., and Clifford D. Shearing. 1996. 'The Future of Policing.' *Law and Society Review* 30: 585–606.

Beare, Margaret E., and George S. Rigakos. 1997. *Interviews with Nine Greater Toronto Area Private Security Executives on Privatization and Overlapping Functions with the Public Police: Raw Data.* North York: York University (unpublished mimeograph available from Margaret E. Beare, Jack and Mae Nathanson Centre for the Study of Organized Crime and Corruption, Osgoode Hall Law School of York University, 4700 Keele St, North York, Ontario, M3J 1P3).

Beck, Ulrich. 1992a. 'Modern society as a risk society.' Pp. 199–214 in *The Culture and Power of Knowledge,* edited by N. Stehr and Richard V. Ericson. Berlin: de Gruyter.

– 1992b. *Risk Society: Towards a New Modernity.* London: Sage.

Becker, Howard S. 1967. 'Whose side are we on?' *Social Problems* 14: 239–47.

Becker, Theodore. 1974. 'The place of private police in society: An area of research for the social sciences.' *Social Problems* 21.

Bell, Daniel. 1973. *The Coming of Post-Industrial Society: A Venture in Social Forecasting.* New York: Basic Books.

Bocklet, R. 1990. 'Police-private security operation.' *Law and Order* 38: 54–9.

Bogard, William. 1996. *The Simulation of Surveillance: Hypercontrol in Telematic Societies.* Cambridge: Cambridge University Press.

Böhme, G., and N. Stehr, eds. 1986. *The Knowledge Society: The Growing Impact of Scientific Knowledge on Social Relations.* Dordrecht: D. Reidl.

Bottom, N.R., and K.R. McCreedy. 1984. 'Private security lectures as part of southeast Florida's police recruit training.' *FBI Law Enforcement Bulletin* 53: 17–19.

Brewer, J. 1980. 'Law and disorder in Stuart and Hanoverian England.' *History Today* January: 18–27.

Brown, Lorne, and Caroline Brown. 1978. *An Unauthorized History of the RCMP.* 2nd ed. Toronto: Lewis and Samuel.

Bugbee, R.M. 1983. 'Sounding the alarm on false alarms.' *The Police Chief* 50: 41–2.

Burchell, Graham, Gordon Colin, and Peter Miller, eds. 1991. *The Foucault Effect: Studies in Governmentality.* Chicago: University of Chicago Press.

Campbell, Gayle, and Bryan Reingold. 1994. 'Private security and public policing in Canada.' *Juristat* 14.

Carchedi, Guglielmo. 1977. *On the Economic Identification of Social Classes.* London: Routledge & Kegan Paul.

Carder, Chris. 1994. 'The right to might: Social policing vs. confrontation.' Pp. 28–31 in *The T.O. Magazine.*

Castel, Robert. 1991. 'From "dangerousness" to risk.' Pp. 281–98 in *The Foucault Effect: Studies in Governmentality,* edited by Graham Burchell, Colin Gordon, and Peter Miller. Chicago: University of Chicago Press.

Chan, Janet. 1996. 'Changing police culture.' *British Journal of Criminology* 36: 109–34.

Christie, Nils. 1986. 'Suitable enemies.' Pp. 42–54 in *Abolitionism: Toward a Non-Repressive Approach to Crime,* edited by H. Bianchi and R. Van Swaaningen. Amsterdam: Free University Press.

– *Crime Control as Industry.* London: Routledge.

Cohen, Stanley. 1985. *Visions of Social Control.* Cambridge: Polity.

– 1987. 'Taking decentralization seriously: Values, visions, and policies.' Pp. 358–83 in *Transcarceration: Essays in the Sociology of Social Control,* edited by John Lowman, Robert J. Menzies, and Ted S. Palys. Aldershot: Gower.

Colquhoun, Patrick. 1800. *Treatise on the Police of the Metropolis,* c. 1798, 6th ed. London: Mawman.

Cooper, Lynn, Elliot Currie, Jon Frappier, Tony Platt, Betty Ryan, Richard Schauffler, Joy Scruggs, and Larry Trujillo, eds. 1975. *The Iron Fist and the Velvet Glove.* Berkeley: Center for Research on Criminal Justice.

Couch, S.R. 1981. 'Selling and reclaiming state sovereignty: The case of the coal and iron police.' *Insurgent Sociologist* 10: 1, 85–91.

Cunningham, W.C., J.J. Strauchs, and C.W. Van Meter. 1990. *Private Security Trends 1970–2000: The Hallcrest II.* MacLean, VA: Hallcrest Systems.

Currie, Dawn, Walter S. DeKeseredy, and Brian D. MacLean. 1992. 'Reconstituting social order and social control: Police accountability in Canada.' In

Re-thinking the Administration of Justice, edited by Dawn Currie and Brian D. MacLean. Halifax: Fernwood.

Currie, Elliot. 1997a. 'Market society and social disorder.' Pp. 37–42 in *Thinking Critically about Crime*, edited by Brian D. Maclean and Dragan Milovanovic. Vancouver: Collective Press.

– 1997b. 'Market, crime and community: Toward a mid-range theory of post-industrial violence.' *Theoretical Criminology* 1: 147–72.

Dandeker, C. 1990. *Surveillance, Power and Modernity: Bureaucracy and Discipline from 1700 to the Present Day*. Cambridge: Polity Press.

Davis, M. 1990. *City of Quartz: Excavating the Future of Los Angeles*. London: Verso.

de Certeau, Michel. 1986. *Heterologies: Discourse on the Other*. Minneapolis: University of Minnesota Press.

Dean, Mitchell. 1994. *Critical and Effective Histories: Foucault's Methods and Historical Sociology*. London: Routledge.

Defert, Daniel. 1991. '"Popular life" and insurance technology.' Pp. 211–34 in *The Foucault Effect: Studies in Governmentality*, edited by Graham Burchell, Colin Gordon, and Peter Miller. Chicago: University of Chicago Press.

DeKeseredy, Walter, and Brian D. MacLean. 1990. 'Discrimination against Native peoples in the Canadian parole process.' Pp. 61–8 in *Racism, Empiricism and Criminal Justice*, edited by Brian D. MacLean and Dragan Milovanovic. Vancouver: Collective Press.

Delucchi, Kevin L. 1983. 'The use and misuse of chi-square: Lewis and Burke revisited.' *Psychological Bulletin* 94: 166–76.

Denzin, N.K. 1978. *Sociological Methods: A Sourcebook*. New York: McGraw-Hill.

Di Matteo, Enzo. 1997. 'Are security guards taking over?' Pp. 18–19, 21 in *Now*. Toronto.

Douglas, M. 1986. *How Institutions Think*. Syracuse: Syracuse University Press.

Ellis, Desmond and Walter S. DeKeseredy. 1996. *The Wrong Stuff*. 2nd. ed. Scarborough: Allyn & Bacon Canada.

Engel, Ume, and Hermann Strasser. 1998. 'Global risks and social inequality: Critical remarks on the risk-society hypothesis.' *Canadian Journal of Sociology* 23(1): 91–103.

Erickson, Bonnie H. 1993. *People Working in the Toronto Private Contract Security Industry*. Ottawa: Police Policy and Research Division Solicitor General of Canada.

Erickson, Bonnie H., Patricia Albanese and Slobodan Drakulic. 2000. 'Gender on a jagged edge: The security industry, its clients, and the reproduction and revision of gender.' *Work and Occupations* 27: 294–318.

Ericson, Richard V. 1982. *Reproducing Order*. Toronto: University of Toronto Press.

– 1994. 'The division of expert knowledge in policing and security.' *British Journal of Sociology* 45: 149–175.

Ericson, Richard V., and Kevin D. Haggerty. 1997. *Policing the Risk Society.* Toronto: University of Toronto Press.

Ericson, Richard V., Kevin D. Haggerty, and Kevin D. Carriere. 1993. 'Community policing as communications policing.' Pp. 37–70 in *Community Policing: Comparative Aspects of Community Oriented Police Work*, edited by Dieter Dölling and Thomas Feltes. Holzkirchen: Felix-Verlag.

Ericson, Richard V., and Clifford D. Shearing. 1986. 'The scientification of ' police work.' Pp. 129–59 in *The Knowledge Society: The Growing Impact of Scientific Knowledge on Social Relations*, edited by G. Böhme and N. Stehr. Dordrecht: D. Reidl.

Eustace, D.D. 1992. *The Centre for Police and Security Studies at York University: A discussion paper.* North York: Calumet College, York University (unpublished mimeograph available from D.D. Eustace, Centre for Police and Security Studies, Room 614, Atkinson College, 4700 Keele St., North York, Ontario, M3J 1P3).

Ewald, Francois. 1991. 'Insurance and risk.' Pp. 197–210 in *The Foucault Effect: Studies in Governmentality*, edited by Graham Burchell, Colin Gordon, and Peter Miller. Chicago: University of Chicago Press.

Ewick, Patricia. 1993. 'Corporate cures: The commodification of social control.' *Studies in Law, Politics, and Society* 13: 137–57.

Feeley, Malcolm, and Johnathan Simon. 1994. 'Actuarial justice: The emerging new criminal law.' Pp. 173–201 in *The Futures of Criminology*, edited by David Nelken. Thousand Oaks: Sage.

Forcese, Dennis P. 1992. *Policing Canadian Society.* Scarborough: Prentice-Hall Canada.

Foucault, Michel. 1972. *The Archaeology of Knowledge*, translated by A.M. Sheridan. New York: Pantheon.

– 1977. *Discipline and Punish.* New York: Vintage Books.

– 1991a. 'Governmentality.' Pp. 87–104 in *The Foucault Effect: Studies in Governmentality*, edited by Graham Burchell, Colin Gordon, and Peter Miller. Chicago: University of Chicago Press.

– 1991b. 'Questions of method.' Pp. 73–86 in *The Foucault Effect: Studies in Governmentality*, edited by Graham Burchell, Colin Gordon, and Peter Miller. Chicago: University of Chicago Press.

Freedman, M.B., and Philip C. Stenning. 1977. *Private Security, Police and the Law in Canada.* Toronto: Centre of Criminology, University of Toronto.

Friedman, D. 1973. *The Machinery of Freedom: A Guide to Radical Capitalism.* New York: Arlington House.

Gabor, Thomas. 1981. 'The crime displacement hypothesis: An empirical examination.' *Crime and Delinquency* 27: 390–404.

Garland, David. 1996. 'The limits of the sovereign state: Strategies of crime control in contemporary society.' *British Journal of Criminology* 36: 445–71.

– 1997. '"Governmentality" and the problem of crime: Foucault, criminology, sociology.' *Theoretical Criminology* 1: 173–214.

Geraghty, Tony. 1986. *March or Die: France and the French Foreign Legion.* Toronto: Grafton.

Giddens, Anthony. 1991. *Modernity and Self-Identity: Self and Society in the Late Modern Age.* Cambridge: Polity Press.

Goffman, Erving. 1961. *Asylums: Essays on the Social Situations of Mental Patients and other Inmates.* New York: Anchor.

Goldstein, Herman. 1990. *Problem-Oriented Policing.* Philadelphia: Temple University Press.

Gordon, P. 1987. 'Community policing: Towards the local police state?' Pp. 121–44 in *Law, Order and the Authoritarian State,* edited by Phil Scraton. Philadelphia: Open University Press.

Greene, Jack. 1997. 'Policing through the prism of business and industry.' Pp. 8–10 in *Measuring What Matters,* edited by Jeremy Travis. Washington: National Institute of Justice.

Greene, J.R., T.M. Seamon, and P.R. Levy. 1995. 'Merging public and private security for collective benefit: Philadelphia's Center City district.' *American Journal of the Police* 14: 3–20.

Hacking, Ian. 1991. 'How should we do the history of statistics?' Pp. 181–95 in *The Foucault Effect: Studies in Governmentality,* edited by Graham Burchell, Colin Gordon, and Peter Miller. Chicago: University of Chicago Press.

Henry, Stuart. 1983. *Private Justice: Towards Integrated Theorizing in the Sociology of Law.* London: Routledge.

Henry, Stuart, and Dragan Milovanovic. 1991. 'Constitutive criminology.' *Criminology* 29: 293–316.

Hertig, C.A. 1986. 'Developing productive realtionships with private security.' *FBI Law Enforcement Bulletin* 55: 19–22.

Hirst, Paul Q. 1973. 'Radical Deviancy Theory and Marxism: A Reply to Taylor and Walton.' Pp. 238–43 in *Critical Criminology,* edited by Ian Taylor, Paul Walton, and Jock Young. London: Routledge.

– 1975. 'Marx and Engels on Law, Crime and Morality.' Pp. 203–32 in *Critical Criminology,* edited by Ian Taylor, Paul Walton, and Jock Young. London: Routledge.

– 1994. *Associative Democracy: New Forms of Economic and Social Governance.* Cambridge: Polity.

Hobbs, Dick and Steve Hall. 1999. *Bouncers: The Art and Economics of Intimidation.* ERSC Research Program Report. No. L133251050.

Hollway, Wendy, and Tony Jefferson. 1997. 'The risk society in an age of anxiety: Situating fear of crime.' *British Journal of Sociology* 48: 255–66.

Hoskins, Frank P. 1997. 'Search and seizure.' Pp. 303–28 in *From Crime to Punishment*, edited by Joel E. Pink and David C. Perrier. Scarborough: Carswell.

Howson, Gerald. 1970. *Thief-Taker General.* London: Hutchison.

Intelligarde. Nd. *Intelligarde: The Law Enforcement Company.* Toronto: author (mimeograph available from Intelligarde International, 55 Unwin Avenue, Toronto, Ontario, M5A 1A2).

Jameson, Fredric. 1984. 'Postmodernism, or the cultural logic of late capitalism.' *New Left Review* 146: 59–92

Johnson, Bruce C. 1976. 'Taking care of labor: The police in American politics.' *Theory and Society* 3: 89–117.

Johnston, Les. 1992. *The Rebirth of Private Policing.* London: Routledge.

– 1996. 'What is vigilantism?' *British Journal of Criminology* 36: 220–36.

– 2000. *Policing Britain: Risk, Security and Governance.* London: Longman.

Jones, Trevor, and Tim Newburn. 1998. *Private Security and Public Policing.* Oxford: Clarendon Press.

– 1995. 'How big is the private security sector?' *Policing and Society* 5: 221–232.

Jurstat. 1997. *Canadian Crime Statistics, 1997.* Ottawa: Canadian Centre for Justice Statistics.

Kakalik, J., and S. Wildhorn. 1971. *Private Police in the United States.* Washington: Government Printing Office.

Kempa, Michael, Ryan Carrier, Jennifer Wood, and Clifford Shearing. 1999. 'Reflections on the evolving concept of "private policing."' *European Journal of Criminal Policy and Research* 7: 197–224.

Klare, M.T. 1975. 'Rent-a-cop: The private security industry in the U.S.' Pp. 104–14 in *The Iron Fist and the Velvet Glove: An Analysis of the U.S. Police*, edited by L. Cooper, E. Currie, J. Frappier, T. Platt, B. Ryan, R. Schauffler, J. Scruggs, and L. Trujillo. Berkeley: Center for Research on Criminal Justice.

Klockars, Carl B. 1988. 'The rhetoric of community policing.' Pp. 239–58 in *Community Policing: Rhetoric or Reality?* edited by Jack R. Greene and Stephen D. Mastroski. New York: Praeger.

Knemeyer, Franz-Ludwig. 1980. 'Polizei.' *Economy and Society* 9(2): 172–96.

Kraska, Peter B., and Victor E. Kappeler. 1997. 'Militarizing American police: The rise and normalization of paramilitary units.' *Social Problems* 44: 1–18.

Kushnirsky, Fyodor I., and William J. Stull. 1989. 'Productive and Unproductive Labour: Smith, Marx, and the Soviets.' In *Perspectives on the History of Economic Thought*, edited by Donald A. Walker. Aldershot: Gower.

Lansdowne, The Marquis of, ed. 1927. *The Petty Papers in Two Volumes*. New York: Augustus M. Kelley.

Lea, John, and Jock Young. 1984. *What Is to Be Done about Law and Order?* Harmondsworth: Penguin.

Leadbeater, David. 1985. 'The consistency of Marx's categories of productive and unproductive labour.' *History of Political Economy* 17: 591–618.

Leclair, Christopher, and Stephen Long. 1996. *The Canadian Security Sector: An Overview*. Toronto: Industrial Adjustment Committee on the Security Sector.

Lee, M. 1991. 'Across the public-private divide? Private policing, grey intelligence and civil actions in local drugs control.' *European Journal of Crime, Criminal Law and Criminal Justice* 3: 381–94.

Lee, W.L.M. 1901. *A History of the Police in England*. London: Methuen.

Leiss, William. 1994. 'Book Review: Risk Society: Towards a New Modernity, by Ulrich Beck.' *Canadian Journal of Sociology* 19: 544–7.

Lenin, Vladimir I. 1952/75. *Imperialism, the Highest Stage of Capitalism*. Peking: Foreign Languages Press.

Lister, Stuart, Dick Hobbs, Steve Hall and Simon Winlow. 2000. 'Violence in the night-time economy; Bouncers: The reporting, recording and prosecution of assaults.' *Policing and Society* 10: 383–402.

Loader, Ian. 1999. 'Consumer culture and the commodification of policing and security.' *Sociology* 33: 373–92.

Lofland, John. 1974. 'Styles of reporting qualitative field research.' *The American Sociologist* 9: 101–11.

Lowi, Theodore. 1990. 'Risks and rights in the history of American governments.' *Daedalus* 119: 17–40.

Lowman, John. 1990. 'Foucault on power: A quick fix.' In *Papers presented at the Conference, Perspectives from Feminism and Foucault*. Burnaby, BC: Simon Fraser University.

Lynch, Michael J., and E.B. Patterson. 1990. 'Racial discrimination in the criminal justice system: Evidence from four jurisdictions.' Pp. 51–60 in *Racism, Empiricism and Criminal Justice*, edited by Brian D. MacLean and Dragan Milovanovic. Vancouver: Collective Press.

Lynch, William. 1996. *Method in the Early Royal Society of London*. PhD dissertation, Cornell University.

Lyon, David. 1994. *The Electronic Eye: The Rise of Surveillance Society*. Minneapolis: University of Minnesota Press.

Mallett, Mick. 1996. 'Police victimization from law and order: Guns and roses on "cops."' *The Criminologist* 21: 1, 6, 8, 10.

Maki, Dennis. 1988. *The Market for Employment, Personnel and Security*. Vancouver: The Fraser Institute.

Mandel, Ernest. 1975. *Late Capitalism*. London: NLB.

Manning, Peter K. 1992. 'Information technologies and the police.' Pp. 349–98 in *Modern Policing*, edited by Michael Tonry and Norval Morris. Chicago: University of Chicago Press.

– 1996. 'Dramas of control: Some anticipated consequences of information technology on loyalty.' Pp. 10–27 in *Vision 2021: Security Issues for the Next Quarter Century*, edited by Theodore R. Sarbin. McLean, VA.

– 1997. *Police Work: The Social Organization of Policing*, 2nd. Prospect Heights: Waveland Press.

Manning, Peter K., and John H. Van Maanen, eds. 1978. *Policing: A View from the Street*. Santa Monica: Goodyear.

Marx, Gary T. 1987. 'The interweaving of public and private police in undercover work.' Pp. 172–93 in *Private Policing*, edited by Clifford D. Shearing and Philip C. Stenning. Newbury Park: Sage.

– 1988. *Undercover: Police Surveillance in America*. Berkeley: University of California Press.

Marx, Gary T., and Nancy Reichman. 1987. 'Routinizing the discovery of secrets: Computers as informants.' Pp. 188–208 in *Transcarceration: Essays in the Sociology of Social Control*, edited by John Lowman, Robert J. Menzies, and Ted S. Palys. Aldershot: Gower.

Marx, Karl. 1970. *Capital*, Vol. III. New York: Independent Publishers.

– 1972a. *Theories of Surplus-Value*, I. London: Lawrence and Wishart.

– 1972b. *Theories of Surplus-Value*, III. London: Lawrence and Wishart.

– 1973. *Grundrisse*, translated and introduced by Martin Nicolaus. New York: Penguin.

– 1976. *Capital*, Vol. I. New York: Penguin Books.

Marx, Karl, and Frederick Engels. 1965. *The German Ideology*, Part II. New York: Lawrence and Wishart.

– 1970a. *The German Ideology*, Part I. edited and introduced by C.J. Arthur. New York: International Publishers.

– 1970b. *Introduction to a Critique of Political Economy*. In Karl Marx and Frederick Engels, *The German Ideology*, supplementary texts, edited and introduced by C.J. Arthur. New York: International Publishers.

McBarnet, D. 1981. *Conviction: Law, the State and the Construction of Justice*. London: Edward Arnold.

McCormick, Kevin R.E., and Livy A. Visano. 1992. 'Policing understanding: Cultural controls and contesting contexts.' Pp. xi–xiii in *Understanding Policing*, edited by Kevin R.E. McCormick and Livy A. Visano. Toronto: Canadian Scholar's Press.

McMullan, John L. 1995. 'The political economy of thief-taking.' *Crime, Law, and Social Change: An International Journal* 23: 121–46.

– 1996. 'Policing, lawlessness, and disorder in historical perspective.' Pp. 111–40 in *Post-Critical Criminology*, edited by Thomas O'Reilly-Fleming. Scarborough: Prentice Hall Canada.

– 1998. 'Social surveillance and the rise of the "police machine."' *Theoretical Criminology: An International Journal* 2: 93–117.

Menzies, Robert J. 1988. 'Beyond realist criminology' Pp. 139–56 in *Realist Criminology: Crime Control and Policing in the 1990s*. Toronto: University of Toronto Press.

Messerschmidt, James W. 1993. *Masculinites and Crime: Critique and Reconceptualization*. Lanham: Rowman & Littlefield.

– 1997. 'Structured action theory: Understanding the interrelation of gender, race, class, and crime.' Pp. 67–74 in *Thinking Critically about Crime*, edited by Brian D. MacLean and Dragan Milovanovic. Vancouver: Collective Press.

Metropolitan Toronto Police Service. 1995a. *1995 Statistics: Companion to the 1995 Annual Report*. Toronto: Author.

– 1995b. 'Environmental Scan.' Toronto: Author (unpublished mimeograph).

– 1996. *Annual Report*. Toronto: author.

– 1998. 'Employment Equity Record Management Report.' Toronto: author (unpublished mimeograph produced by Corporate Communication Office, Metropolitan Toronto Police Service, 14 January 1998).

Miccuci, Anthony J. 1995. 'Changing of the guard: The transformation of private security.' *Journal of Security Administration* 18: 21–45.

– *The Changing of the Guard: A Case Study of Professionalization in a Campus Security Force*. PhD dissertation, Department of Sociology, York University. North York.

Miller, Peter, and Nikolas Rose. 1995. 'Political thought and the limits of orthodoxy: A response to Curtis.' *British Journal of Sociology* 46: 590–7.

– 1997. 'Mobilizing the consumer: Assembling the subject of consumption.' *Theory, Culture, & Society* 14: 1–36.

Mitchell, Bob. 1990a. 'Firms on the alert for false alarms.' *Toronto Star*. W8 Toronto.

– 'Security firms bullish on cutting false alarms.' *Toronto Star* N1.

Moulton, R. 1987. 'Should private security have access to criminal conviction files?' *The Police Chief* 54: 35.

Murphy, Chris. 1988. 'Community problems, problem communities, and community policing in Toronto.' *Journal of Research in Crime and Delinquency* 25: 392–410.

Newburn, T., and Elizabeth Stanko, eds. 1994. *Just Boys Doing Business? Men, Masculinities and Crime*. London: Routledge.

Normandeau, André, and Barry Leighton. 1990. *A Vision of the Future of Policing in Canada: Police-Challenge 2000.* Ottawa: Solicitor General Canada.

OCAP. 1997 (8 May). 'Intelligarde's Assault on the Poor.' Toronto: Ontario Coalition Against Poverty (unpublished mimeograph available from the Ontario Coalition Against Poverty, 1249 Sherbourne Street, Toronto, Ontario, M5A 2R9).

O'Leary, D. 1994. 'Reflections on police privatization.' *FBI Law Enforcement Bulletin* 63: 21–5.

O'Malley, Pat. 1991. 'Legal networks and domestic security.' *Studies in Law, Politics, and Society* 11: 171–90.

– 1992. 'Risk, power and crime prevention.' *Economy and Society* 21: 252–75.

– 1993. 'Containing our excitement: Commodity culture and the crisis of discipline.' *Studies in Law, Politics, and Society* 13: 159–86.

– 1996. 'Risk and responsibility.' Pp. 189–207 in *Foucault and Political Reason: Liberalism, Neo-liberalism, and Rationalities of Government,* edited by Andrew Berry, Thomas Osborne, and Nikolas Rose. London: UCL Press.

– 2001. 'Discontinuity, government and risk: A response to Rigakos and Hadden.' *Theoretical Criminology* 5: 85–92.

O'Malley, Pat, and Darren Palmer. 1996. 'Post-Keynesian policing.' *Economy and Society* 25: 137–55.

O'Malley, Pat, Lorna Weir, and Clifford Shearing. 1997. 'Governmentality, criticism, politics.' *Economy and Society* 26: 501–17.

O'Toole, G. 1978. *The Private Sector: Private Spies, Rent-a-Cops, and the Police-Industrial Complex.* New York: W.W. Norton.

Palango, Paul. 1998. 'On the mean streets: As the police cut back, private cops are moving in.' Pp. 10–14 in *Maclean's.*

Palys, Ted. 1992. *Research Decisons: Quantitative and Qualitative Perspectives.* Toronto: Harcourt Brace Jovanovich.

Pancake, D. 1983. 'The new professionals: Cooperation between police departments and private security.' *The Police Chief* 50: 34–6.

Peterson, H.I. 1983. 'Private security v. public law enforcement.' *The Police Chief* 50: 26–7.

Pfohl, Stephen. 1985. *Images of Deviance and Social Control.* New York: McGraw-Hill.

Poster, Mark. 1990. *The Mode of Information.* Chicago: University of Chicago Press.

Pratt, Laura. 1995. 'Top paracops.' Pp. 53, 55–8 in *Toronto Life.*

Priest, George L. 1990. 'The new legal structure of risk control.' *Daedulus* 119: 207–27.

Reichman, Nancy. 1986. 'Managing crime risks: Toward an insurance based model of social control.' *Research in Law, Deviance and Social Control* 8: 151–72.

Reiman, Jefferey. 1995. *The Rich Get Richer and the Poor Get Prison*. Needham Heights: Allyn & Bacon.

Reiner, Robert. 1978. 'The police in the class structure.' *British Journal of Law and Society* 5: 166–84.

– 1992. *The Politics of the Police*, 2nd. Toronto: University of Toronto Press.

Rigakos, George S. 1995. 'Constructing the symbolic complainant: Police subculture and the nonenforcement of protection orders for battered women.' *Violence and Victims* 10: 227–47.

– 1997a. 'Community policing: A critical meta-analytic research brief.' Pp. 28–38 in *Policing the New Millenium: Critical Essays on Social Control*, edited by Critical Criminology Association at York University. North York: Centre for Police and Security Studies, York University.

– 1997b. 'The politics of crime control in a risk society.' Paper presented at the annual meetings of the Society for the Study of Social Problems. Toronto, 28 August.

– 1998. 'Book review: *The Simulation of Surveillance*, by William Bogard, Cambridge University Press, 1996.' *Justice Quarterly* 15: 567–72.

– 1999. 'Risk society and actuarial criminology: Prospects for a critical discourse.' *Canadian Journal of Criminology* 41: 137–50.

– 2001. 'On continuity, risk and political economy: A response to O'Malley.' *Theoretical Criminology* 5(1): 93–100.

Rigakos, George, and David Greener. 2000. 'Bubbles of Governance: Private Policing and the Law in Canada.' *Canadian Journal of Law and Society* 15: 145–85.

Rigakos, George S., and Richard W. Hadden. 2001. 'Crime, capitalism and the "risk society:" Towards the same olde modernity?' *Theoretical Criminology* 5: 61–84.

Rose, Nikolas. 1996. 'The death of the social? Re-figuring the territory of government.' *Economy and Society* 25: 327–56.

Rose, Nikolas, and Peter Miller. 1992. 'Political power beyond the state: Problematics of government.' *British Journal of Sociology* 43: 173–205.

Rothbard, M.N. 1978. *For a New Liberty: The Libertarian Manifesto*. New York: Collier MacMillan.

Rustin, Michael. 1994. 'Incomplete modernity: Ulrich Beck's *Risk Society*.' *Radical Philosophy* 67: 3–19.

Rygier, P. 1983. 'Shopping mall precinct Deptford Township.' *The Police Chief* 50: 38.

Sarre, R. 1994. 'Legal powers of private police and security providers.' pp. 259–80 in *Private Prisons and Police: Recent Australian Trends*, edited by Paul Moyle. Leichhardt, NSW: Pluto Press.

Schwartz, Martin D., and Dragan Milovanovic. 1996. *Race, Gender and Class: The Intersection.* New York: Garland.

Seidman, Steven, and David G. Wagner, eds. 1992. *Postmodernism and Social Theory: The Debate over General Theory.* Cambridge, MA: Blackwell.

Shearing, Clifford D. 1992. 'The relations between public and private policing.' Pp. 399–434 in *Modern Policing*, edited by Michael Tonry and Norval Morris. Chicago: University of Chicago Press.

– 1993. 'Policing: Relationships between public and private.' Pp. 203–27 in *Alternative Policing Styles: Cross-Cultural Perspectives*, edited by Mark Findlay and Zvekic Uglješa. Boston: Kluwer Law and Taxation Publishers (United Nations Interregional Crime and Justice Research Institute).

– 1997. 'Unrecognized origins of the new policing: Linkages between private and public policing.' Pp. 219–30 in *Business and Crime Prevention*, edited by Marcus Felson and Ronald V. Clarke. Monsey, NY: Criminal Justice Press.

– 'Punishment and the Changing face of governance.' *Punishment and Society.* Forthcoming.

Shearing, Clifford D., Margaret B. Farnell, and Philip C. Stenning. 1980. *Contract Security in Ontario.* Toronto: Centre of Criminology, University of Toronto.

Shearing, Clifford D., and Philip C. Stenning. 1982a. *Private Security and Justice: The Challenge of the 80s.* Montreal: The Institute for Research on Public Policy.

– 1982b. 'Snowflakes or good pinches? – Private security's contribution to modern policing.' Pp. 96–110 in *Maintenance of Order in Society*, edited by Rita Donelan. Ottawa: Ministry of Supply and Services.

– 1983. 'Private security: Implications for social control.' *Social Problems* 30: 498–505.

– 1987a. 'Reframing policing.' Pp. 9–18 in *Private Policing*, edited by Clifford D. Shearing and Philip C. Stenning. Newbury Park: Sage.

– 1987b. 'SAY "CHEESE:" The Disney order that is not so Mickey Mouse.' Pp. 317–23 in *Private Policing*, edited by Clifford D. Shearing and Philip C. Stenning. Newbury Park: Sage.

Shearing, Clifford D., Philip C. Stenning, and Susan M. Addario. 1985a. 'Corporate perceptions of private security.' *Canadian Police College Journal* 9: 367–90.

– 1985b. 'Police perceptions of private security.' *Canadian Police College Journal* 9: 127–53.

– 1985c. 'Public perceptions of private security.' *Canadian Police College Journal* 9: 225–53.

Simon, Johnathan. 1987. 'The emergence of a risk society: Insurance, law, and the state.' *Socialist Review* 95: 61–89.

– 1988. 'The ideological effects of actuarial practices.' *Law & Society Review* 22: 773–99.

– 1994. *Poor Discipline*. Chicago: University of Chicago Press.

Skolnick, Jerome. 1966. *Justice without Trial*. New York: Wiley and Sons.

Smith, Adam. 1937. *An Inquiry into the Wealth of Nations*. New York: Modern Library.

Smith, D.J., and J. Gray. 1983. *The Police in Action*. London: Policy Studies Institute.

Solicitor General Canada. 1996. *Partners in Policing: The Royal Canadian Mounted Police Contract Policing Program*. Ottawa: Solicitor General Canada, Policing Directorate (e-text available from www.sgc.ca/epub/pol/e199690/ e199690.htm, or visit www.sgc.ca/ehome.htm).

South, Nigel. 1984. 'Private security, the division of policing labor and the commercial compromise of the state.' *Research in Law, Deviance and Social Control* 6: 171–98.

– 1987. 'Law, profit, and "private persons:" Private and public policing in English history.' Pp. 72–109 in *Private Policing*, edited by Clifford D. Shearing and Philip C. Stenning. Newbury Park: Sage.

– 1988. *Policing for Profit*. London: Sage.

Spitzer, Steven. 1981. 'The political economy of policing.' pp. 314–41 in *Crime and Capitalism: Readings in Marxist Criminology*, edited by David F. Greenberg. Palo Alto: Mayfield.

– 1987. 'Security and control in capitalist societies: The fetishism of security and the secret thereof.' Pp. 43–58 in *Transcarceration: Essays in the Sociology of Social Control*, edited by John Lowman, Robert J. Menzies, and Ted S. Palys. Aldershot: Gower.

Spitzer, Steven, and Andrew T. Scull. 1977. 'Privatization and capitalist development.' *Social Problems* 25: 18–29.

Stemman, Roy. 1997. 'Group 4 in demand in Australia.' Pp. 10–11 in *Group 4 Securitas: International Magazine*. The Hague: Group 4 Securitas.

Stenning, Philip C. 1997. 'Reclaiming the Policing Agenda – A Proposal for Change.' Toronto: Submission to the Anti-Racism, Access and Equity Committee, Metro Toronto Council.

Stenning, Philip C., and Clifford D. Shearing. 1979. *Powers of Security Personnel*. Ottawa: Law Reform Commission of Canada.

Thomas, Jim. 1993. *Doing Critical Ethnography*. Newbury Park: Sage.

Trojanowicz, Robert J. and B. Bucqueroux. 1990. *Community Policing: A Contemporary Perspective*. Cincinnati: Anderson.

Wagner, David G. 1984. *The Growth of Sociological Theories*. Beverly Hills: Sage.

Weiss, Robert. 1978. 'The emergence and transformation of private detective

industrial policing in the United States, 1850–1940.' *Crime & Social Justice* 9:
35–48.

Westley, W. 1970. *Violence and the Police.* Cambridge: MIT Press.

Wilson, James Q. and George L. Kelling. 1982. 'Broken windows.' *Atlantic
Monthly* March: 29–38.

Index